Harvard Business Review

ON

COMPENSATION

THE HARVARD BUSINESS REVIEW PAPERBACK SERIES

The series is designed to bring today's managers and professionals the fundamental information they need to stay competitive in a fast-moving world. From the preeminent thinkers whose work has defined an entire field to the rising stars who will redefine the way we think about business, here are the leading minds and landmark ideas that have established the *Harvard Business Review* as required reading for ambitious businesspeople in organizations around the globe.

Other books in the series:

Harvard Business Review Interviews with CEOs

Harvard Business Review on Brand Management

Harvard Business Review on Breakthrough Thinking

Harvard Business Review on Business and the Environment

Harvard Business Review on the Business Value of IT

Harvard Business Review on Change

Harvard Business Review on Corporate Governance

Harvard Business Review on Corporate Strategy

Harvard Business Review on Crisis Management

Harvard Business Review on Decision Making

Harvard Business Review on Effective Communication

Harvard Business Review on Entrepreneurship

Harvard Business Review on Finding and Keeping the Best People

Harvard Business Review on Innovation

Harvard Business Review on Knowledge Management

Harvard Business Review on Leadership

Harvard Business Review on Managing High-Tech Industries

Harvard Business Review on Managing People

Harvard Business Review on Managing Diversity

Harvard Business Review

ON

COMPENSATION

A HARVARD BUSINESS REVIEW PAPERBACK

The *Harvard Business Review* articles in this collection are available as
individual reprints. Discounts apply to quantity purchases. For information and ordering, please contact Customer Service, Harvard Business
School Publishing, Boston, MA 02163. Telephone: (617) 783-7500 or
(800) 988-0886, 8 A.M. to 6 P.M. Eastern Time, Monday through Friday.
Fax: (617) 783-7555, 24 hours a day. E-mail: custserv@hbsp.harvard.edu

Library of Congress Cataloging-in-Publication Data
Harvard business review on compensation.
     p.   cm. — (A Harvard business review paperback)
   Includes bibliographical references and index.
     ISBN 1-57851-701-X (alk. paper)
     1. Compensation management.   2. Wages and labor productivity.
3. Employee fringe benefits.   4. Executives—Salaries, etc.   5. Wages.
6. Labor economics.   I. Title: Compensation.   II. Harvard Business
School Press.   III. Harvard business review.   IV. Harvard business
review paperback series.
HF5549.5.C67 H37 2002
658.3´2—dc21   2001039851
                                                                        CIP

*The paper used in this publication meets the requirements of the Ameri-
can National Standard for Permanence of Paper for Publications and
Documents in Libraries and Archives Z39.48-1992.*

Contents

Harvard Business Review

ON

COMPENSATION

New Thinking on How to Link Executive Pay with Performance

ALFRED RAPPAPORT

Executive Summary

AS THE STOCK MARKET began its ascent in the mid-1990s, executive pay—always the subject of heated debate—mounted along with it. That's because among the largest U.S. companies, stock options now account for more then half of total CEO compensation and about 30% of senior operating managers' pay. One problem became particularly clear during the bull market's astonishing run: even below-average performers reap huge gains form stock options when the market is rising rapidly.

The author proposes steps to close the gap between existing compensation practices and those needed to promote higher levels of achievement at all levels of the corporation.

For top managers, he recommends replacing conventional stock options with options that are tied to a market or peer index. Below-average performers would not be rewarded under such plans; superior performers could, depending on the way plans were structured, receive even more. He notes that managers at the business unit level should not be judged on the company's stock price—over which they have little control—and advocates an approach that accurately measures the value added by each unit. Finally, he suggests how certain indicators of value can be used to measure the contribution of front-line managers and employees.

The concept of pay for performance has gained wide acceptance, but the link between incentive pay and superior performance is still too weak. Reforms must be adopted at all levels of the organization. Shareholders will applaud changes in pay schemes that motivate companies to deliver more value.

T HE TOPIC OF executive compensation generates heated discussion. And, because stock options have become the fastest growing segment of executive pay, performance-related pay in particular attracts high-decibel debate. Stock options now account for more than half of total CEO compensation in the largest U.S. companies and about 30% of senior operating managers' pay. Options and stock grants also constitute almost half of directors' remuneration.

This trend is relatively new. The takeover movement of the 1980s provided a powerful incentive for companies to introduce compensation schemes tied directly to stock prices. Before that, executive pay was largely a matter of salaries and of bonuses that were paid out only if financial targets were met. It was widely thought that a company's stock price correlated with its ability to meet certain financial goals. A number of studies, however, cast doubt on the supposed relationship between bonuses, financial targets, and stock prices. For example, Michael C. Jensen and Kevin J. Murphy's often cited HBR article "CEO Incentives—It's Not How Much You Pay, But How" (May–June 1990) showed that there was virtually no link between how much CEOs were paid and how well their companies performed for shareholders.

In the early 1990s, corporate boards began to highlight shareholder value. They became convinced that the surest way to align the interests of managers with those of shareholders was to make stock options a large component of executive compensation. By the mid-1990s, CEOs and other senior managers found themselves with significant stock and options holdings.

The huge gains from options for below-average performers should give pause to even the most ardent defender of current corporate pay systems.

As the stock market began its ascent, executive pay mounted. But the correlation between a CEO's pay and the stock market did not prove that a company was enjoying superior performance: when the market is rising, stock options reward both superior and subpar performance.

That's because *any* increase in a company's share price constitutes "positive performance" with conventional stock options. Any increase in share price will reward the holder of a stock option without distinguishing between good performance and bad. The almost 100% increase in major stock market indexes between 1995 and 1997 exposed this shortcoming. Executives with fixed-price options enjoyed a huge windfall from the long-running bull market that was fueled not only by corporate performance but also by factors beyond management control, such as declining inflation and lower interest rates.

How easy is it to earn a positive return when the stock market is rising? For the ten-year period ending in 1997, total return to shareholders—dividends plus increases in the share price—was positive for each of the 100 largest U.S. companies. The huge gains from options for below-average performers should give pause to even the most ardent defender of current corporate pay systems.

Fortunately, the gap between existing compensation practices and those needed to promote higher levels of achievement can be bridged. In doing so, all levels of the corporation, not just the top, must be considered. The ultimate goal of providing superior total returns to shareholders can be better accomplished by following three steps: first, by rewarding top managers only when they outperform the competition; second, by determining the real contribution of each business unit to the company's overall share price; and third, by involving frontline managers and workers in the quest for higher shareholder value. We'll examine how each of these steps can be carried out.

Problems with Pay at the Top

For incentive compensation to work, corporate boards must choose both the right measures and the right levels of performance. In principle, stock options employ the right measure of performance for corporate executives who are responsible for the company as a whole. After all, the value of a stock option is driven by the share price, which is the largest component of shareholders' total return. Some managers protest that shareholders' expectations are unrealistically high, but the weight of evidence does not support that conclusion.

Surveys, for example—whether taken in rising or falling markets—consistently and overwhelmingly report that most CEOs believe their company's shares are undervalued. Companies are backing up this belief by repurchasing shares at record levels—and studies show that stock prices respond positively to announcements of repurchased shares. In addition, forecasted performance in a company's own long-term business plans is frequently well above the level needed to justify its current stock price. Finally, companies are increasingly using stock to finance acquisitions. Executives dedicated to increasing shareholder value would not do that if they believed that shares were undervalued. Most CEOs, in short, place a lot of stock in their company's share price.

Fixed-price options reward executives for any increase in share price— even if the increase is well below that realized by competitors.

If stock options set the right measure of executive performance, do they also set the right level? The answer is no. Shareholders expect boards to reward management for achieving superior returns—that is, for returns equal to or better than those earned by the company's peer group or by broader market indexes. That is how institutional investors distinguish performing from underperforming companies and also how the *Wall Street Journal* "Shareholder Scoreboard" compares performance in its annual rankings of the 1,000 largest U.S. companies. To help investors monitor executive pay, the Securities and Exchange Commission even requires companies in their annual executive compensation disclosure to report the total return to shareholders relative to their peers or to the market as a whole. But although many boards and CEOs publicly acknowledge the paramount importance of delivering superior returns to shareholders, current stock option schemes reward both mediocre and superior performance. In other words, boards are not setting the right level of performance.

The problem lies in the way conventional stock options are structured. The exercise price is established at the market price on the day the options are granted and stays fixed over the entire option period, usually ten years. If the share price rises above the exercise price, the option holder can cash in on the gains. Therefore, fixed-price options reward executives for any increase in share price—even if the increase is well below that realized by competitors or by the market as a whole.

Consider the following example. A CEO is granted options exercisable over the next ten years on 1 million shares at the current share price of $100. If the share price rises by 5% a year to $163 at the end of the period, the CEO will take home a gain of $63 million. But if the share prices of competitors grow at 15% a year during the same period, a convincing argument can be made that the CEO does not deserve to cash in the options. No reasonable board of directors would knowingly approve a plan that offers high rewards for such poor long-term performance.

Some stock option plans do target a higher level of performance than standard fixed-price options. Companies such as Colgate-Palmolive, Monsanto, and Transamerica, for example, have recently introduced premium-priced stock option plans. In those plans, exercise prices are fixed at a premium above the market price on the date the options are granted, and they remain at that level throughout the life of the options. The premium is usually 25%, 50%, or even 100% of the market price. At those higher exercise prices, the share price for a ten-year option must rise about 2%, 4%, and 7% respectively each year if the option is to be exercised profitably when it expires. But those rates are still well below historical equity returns and investor expectations. More to the point, because the exercise prices remain fixed, premium-priced options hold no guarantee that the level of performance will be superior. During a period of rising markets, premium-priced options may still reward below-average performance. They also offer little or no reward to executives who outperform their competitors during times of modestly rising or declining markets.

The Advantages of Indexing

Stock option plans don't have to be blunt instruments. By tying a plan's exercise price to a selected index, boards can increase the pay of superior performers while appropriately penalizing poor ones. Let's assume the exercise price of a CEO's options are reset each year to reflect changes in a benchmarked index. If the index increases by 15% during the first year, the exercise price of the option would also increase by that amount. The option would then be worth exercising only if the company's shares had gone up by more than 15%. The CEO, therefore, is rewarded only if his or her company outperforms the index.

In selecting an index, companies can choose either an index of their competitors or a broader market index such as the Standard & Poor's 500. The choice requires trade-offs. Stock options indexed to the market are easily measured and tracked. A market index, however, ignores the special factors that affect the company's industry. Although the S&P 500 index has risen spectacularly over the past few years, industries such as steel, heavy construction, pollution control, and paper products have done poorly in comparison. It is better to judge management's contribution using a peer group index. However, because many companies have diversified into a wide range of products and markets, it is sometimes difficult to identify a group of peers.

Whatever index is selected, indexed options have clear advantages over fixed-price options. Indexed options do not reward underperforming executives simply because the market is rising. Nor do they penalize superior performers because the market is declining. They can keep executives motivated not only in the bull markets everyone has grown accustomed to but also in sustained bear markets. They link pay to superior performance in all markets.

Despite their merits, indexed options are likely to meet with opposition. Some objections are rooted in misplaced concerns; others are more fundamental. (See "Misplaced Concerns About Indexed Options" at the end of this article.) Underperforming executives are likely to balk at the more exacting performance standards of indexed options. Indeed, companies committed to providing superior returns to their shareholders will need to carefully consider how switching to indexed options will affect the motivation of their senior managers. In addition, board members, who now receive almost half their compensation in stock grants and fixed-price options, must be persuaded to agree to the same standards for themselves if they are to credibly ask management to accept indexed options.

To persuade executives to accept indexed option packages, the packages should be structured so that

exceptional performers can earn greater returns than
they could with conventional options. Two incentives
need to be incorporated into the packages. First, companies should increase the number of options they grant to
executives; second, they should lower the exercise price.
By taking those actions, boards can get senior managers
to tie their pay to superior performance.

They would be able to do so because the managers
would come out on top with such a plan. The evidence
comes from a study conducted by L.E.K. Consulting,
which examined the performance between 1988 and
1997 of 170 companies in 23 industries represented in
the Dow Jones index. The study found that executives at
two-thirds of superior-performing companies would
have earned more with indexed options structured along
the lines recommended here than they actually did.

Increasing the Options.   To compensate executives for
bearing higher risk, boards will need to offer them more
options. To decide how many more, they first need to
know how many indexed options would offer the same
value as the conventional options that top managers currently possess. I call this number the "value ratio." Take a
typical situation for a company whose share price is
$100. As calculated by option-pricing models, the esti-
mated value of a conventional stock option is $34.50, and
the value of an indexed option is $21.60. The value ratio
is then 34.50 divided by 21.60, or 1.6.

The value ratio is affected principally by changes in
interest rates, stock price volatility, and the correlation
between the chosen index and the stock price. Research
conducted by the University of Toronto's John Hull
has shown that although value ratios are sensitive to
these factors, in most situations they can be expected
to fall in a range of approximately 1.5 to 2.0. But in a

competitive market for top management talent, many
executives are unlikely to be convinced by such figures
and will probably demand more options than the ratios
would suggest. Thus in order to entice executives to
convert, boards must start by offering them at least two
indexed options for every fixed-price option in their
current plan.

Although many CEOs may be reluctant to shift to a
new compensation plan, high-performing ones will do
better with indexed options than with conventional
options if they convert at a two-for-one rate. Suppose, for
example, that a company's stock price was $100 on the
day the options were granted and that a peer index was
established that had the same price. Over ten years, the
index grows at an average of 10% per year and its price
reaches $259. The company, meanwhile, grows by 20%
annually so that its share price reaches $619. The profit
on each indexed option would be $619 minus $259, or
$360, while the gain for a fixed-priced option would be
$619 minus $100, or $519. If two indexed options had
been granted for each fixed-priced option, the gain from
the indexed option package would be $720—that's 39%
greater than the $519 from the fixed-priced option. (To
gauge the impact of different scenarios, see the table
"How Much Can Senior Managers Gain from Indexed
Options?")

Lowering the Exercise Price. By offering two or more
new options for each old one, companies will enable
superior executives to earn even more. But only about
50% of executives can be above average. What about
incentives for the others? One response is that they don't
deserve incentive compensation. On the other hand, it's
probably not in the best interest of shareholders to have

a group of company executives who are less motivated than they could be because their indexed options are presently worthless.

One way to resolve the dilemma is to lower the exercise price for indexed options. There are several ways to do that. The most effective and easiest way is to grant what I call "discounted indexed options"—options whose exercise prices are discounted by some specified rate. A discounted indexed option guarantees an index-generated exercise price while simultaneously allowing managers to profit at a performance level that is

---

How Much Can Senior Managers Gain from Indexed Options?

Superior managers will usually do better with indexed option packages than with conventional packages. And the better a company does relative to the index, the higher the gains. My research also shows that gains from indexed options relative to fixed-price options decrease if options are exercised early. Indexed options thereby encourage managers to stay for the long term.

Number of indexed options granted for each fixed-price option	Annual growth of company's stock price minus the index's growth*		
	5%	10%	15%
2.00	-5	39	62
2.50	19	73	102
3.00	43	108	142

Percentage gains for senior managers on an indexed plan in comparison with a fixed-price plan

*The selected index is assumed to grow 10% annually, a rate that approximates the market's long-term price appreciation.

modestly below the company's peer group average. Discounted indexed options sweeten the package.

To see how such options would work, imagine a company whose board wants to issue them. The board could discount the selected index by a specified rate each year over the life of the option. For example, if in the first year the index rises from $100 to $120, a 1% discount would decrease the year-end index from $120 to $118.80. Thus the exercise price of the stock would have risen by only 18.8% instead of 20%. This approach makes gains from indexed options accessible to more executives. Discounting options also provides further economic motivation for high-performing executives to remain with the company and to hold on to their options. By the end of the ten-year life of the typical option, the cumulative discount on the price of the index would be 10%.

Two additional questions must be answered before CEOs and other senior executives are likely to endorse an indexed option plan. First, how large does the spread have to be between the growth in a company's share price and the index price before the gains from indexed options exceed those from standard ones? In other words, by how much does a company have to outperform its peers? And second, how difficult is it for companies to reach and surpass the break-even spread?

Those questions can be answered by referring to the L.E.K. Consulting study mentioned above. The research shows that a company should outperform its selected index by about 5.4% for two indexed options to generate greater gains than one fixed-price option. That figure falls to about 3.9% if one introduces an annual 1% discount to the indexed options. How easy is it to achieve those spreads? Easier than might be expected. The table "How Many Winners with Indexed Options?" shows, for example, that executives at 64% of the superior-performing companies in the study would have gained if they had exchanged each conventional option for 2.5 indexed options discounted at 1%.

This research, of course, was conducted at a time when the stock market was rising very quickly. The average annual price growth of the S&P 500 index between 1988 and 1997 was 14.7%; the figure was 8.7% for the past 50 years. Would the percentages in the table be affected if price appreciation over the next ten years mirrored the longer-term average? The most reasonable guess is that

---

How Many Winners with Indexed Options?

Discounting options and increasing the value ratio makes it easier for companies to reach the break-even spread—the figure that allows holders of indexed option packages to equal the gains they would have obtained under fixed-price plans. The table shows the percentage of superior-performing companies from a total sample of 170 that would have surpassed the break-even spread for different types of indexed option packages.

Number of indexed options granted for each fixed-price option	Annual discount from 1988 through 1997		
	0%	1%	2%
2.00	29	43	64
2.50	45	64	80
3.00	55	75	88

Percentage of superior-performing companies whose senior managers would have gained more with indexed options than they would have with fixed-price options

the percentages would not change significantly. Although the size of break-even spreads is affected by the overall growth of the market or the selected index, the number of companies that reach or exceed that spread is not affected by the state of the market. In the 23 industries looked at in the study, increases in share price ranged on average from 4% to 24% per year over the ten-year period. I could find no relationship between those figures and the percentage of companies whose executives would have realized greater gains from indexed options than from fixed-price options. This suggests that discounted indexed options will provide a better deal for most managers regardless of stock market conditions.

Judging the Value of Business Units

While CEO pay draws intense interest, the compensation of operating managers is far less scrutinized. It is, however, equally critical to the success of public companies. After all, the primary source of a company's value lies in its operating units. In decentralized companies that have a range of products and markets, operating executives make the important day-to-day decisions and investments. The way those executives are evaluated and paid affects their

Granting stock options to business unit managers is even less a guarantee of performance than it is for CEOs.

behavior and the business's results. In order to close the gaps between pay and performance at the operating unit level, performance targets and incentive pay must be aligned with the interests of shareholders. Otherwise, CEOs will find it difficult to achieve gains from indexed options.

Corporate managers are well aware of the importance of motivating operating managers. Performance packages are now the dominant part of the compensation mix at the operating level. Pearl Meyer & Partners, a consulting firm that specializes in executive compensation, reported that for group heads managing businesses with annual revenues of less than $1 billion, stock options constituted 27% of their compensation packages in 1997. Annual and long-term incentive schemes accounted for a further 41%. Unfortunately, these performance schemes were all based on the wrong measure and wrong level of performance.

Challenges of Measurement and Level. Both boards and the public have generally believed that granting stock options would successfully align the interests of operating unit managers and shareholders. But granting options to such managers is even less a guarantee of performance than it is for CEOs. That's because a company's stock price is not an appropriate measure of the performance of an individual business unit. Business units are essentially private companies embedded in publicly traded companies. The managers of operating units usually have a limited impact on the company's overall success or on its stock price. Incentives based on the share price will not give them the rewards they deserve. A stock price that declines because of disappointing performance in other parts of the company may unfairly penalize the executives of a superior-performing operating unit. On the other hand, if an operating unit performs poorly but the company's shares rise because of superior performance by other units, the executives of that unit will enjoy an unearned windfall. Only when operating units are substantially interdependent can the share price be a fair and useful guide to operating performance.

One can find measures in other incentive schemes that focus better on operating unit performance but are unreliably linked to superior performance. The most frequently employed financial measures include operating income, return on invested capital (ROIC), and return on equity (ROE). Earnings measures are not reliably linked to shareholder value because they do not incorporate the cost of capital and may be calculated using different accounting methods that can produce different numbers. ROIC and ROE have similar accounting shortcomings.

A growing number of companies have also embraced residual income measures, such as economic value added, which deduct a cost of capital charge from earnings. The resulting calculation is thought to be a good estimate of the value added by the business, but these measures also suffer from accounting problems. The most important problem, however, is that schemes using residual income measures typically set too low a level of minimum performance. This conclusion may surprise many managers. It is well established that management creates value when the returns on corporate investments are greater than the cost of capital. But that does not mean operating executives should be rewarded for *any* value created. Using the cost-of-capital standard as a threshold for incentive compensation ignores the level of added value already implied by a company's stock price.

Imagine a corporation whose cost of capital is 10%. The price of its shares reflects investors' belief that the company will find opportunities to invest and operate at an average expected rate of return on investment of 20%. If managers start to invest in projects yielding less, say 15%, investors will revise their expectations downward and the company's shares will fall correspondingly. Few would argue that a manager should be rewarded for such performance, even though he has exceeded the cost of capital.

How often does this gap occur between expected return on investment and the cost of capital? Although the differences vary widely from one industry to another, the share prices of virtually all publicly traded companies reflect the expectation that they will generate returns well above the cost of capital. According to a study by L.E.K. Consulting, for example, the median baseline value for the 100 largest nonfinancial companies is approximately 30% of their stock price. In other words, if investors expected these companies to earn returns at the cost of capital, their shares would be priced at about 70% below current levels. (See the table "Expected Rates of Return Compared with Costs of Capital.")

The Superior Shareholder-Value-Added Approach. How is pay to be set using the right measure at the right level in a business unit? The best way is by valuing a unit as if it were a stand-alone business. The parent's share price, after all, largely reflects the aggregate expectations of its operating units. One way to evaluate business units is by considering "shareholder value added." SVA has one clear advantage over residual income measures: it is based entirely on cash flows and does not introduce accounting distortions. It can therefore serve as a sound basis for an incentive pay plan.

SVA puts a value on changes in the future cash flows of a company or business unit. It is calculated by applying standard discounting techniques to forecasts of operating cash flows for a specific period and then subtracting the incremental future investments anticipated for

Expected Rates of Return Compared with Costs of Capital

*Credit Suisse First Boston, using their own value-driver estimates,
including the cost of capital, calculated the expected or minimum rates
of return on investment needed to justify September 1998 share prices for
the Dow Jones industrial companies. In every case, the expected returns
were greater than the cost of capital.*

The potential for undeserved payment is very high when cost of capital is the threshold. That is as true for business units as it is for corporations, and it applies whenever performance is based on accounting or residual income measures. That's because those measures rely on a company's historical investment rather than on the benchmark against which investors properly measure their returns—the company's current market value.

	Expected Return	Cost of Capital	Difference
Coca-Cola	24.8%	8.8%	16.0%
Merck	22.8	8.9	13.9
General Electric	21.7	9.0	12.7
Johnson & Johnson	21.3	9.1	12.2
AT&T	19.3	8.4	10.9
Caterpillar	19.0	9.0	10.0
J.P. Morgan	18.6	9.0	9.6
Wal-Mart	18.1	8.5	9.6
Philip Morris	17.7	8.4	9.3
DuPont	16.8	8.1	8.7
Boeing	16.6	8.4	8.2
Procter & Gamble	16.5	8.9	7.6
IBM	16.4	7.7	8.7
General Motors	16.2	9.0	7.2
Hewlett-Packard	16.0	8.7	7.3
Eastman Kodak	15.5	8.2	7.3
Disney	13.9	8.2	5.7

Expected Rates of Return Compared with Costs of Capital
(continued)

	Expected Return	Cost of Capital	Difference
United Technologies	13.9	8.9	5.0
AlliedSignal	13.5	8.0	5.5
3M	13.3	8.6	4.7
Travelers Group	12.5	8.6	3.9
McDonald's	12.2	7.5	4.7
Alcoa	12.2	8.4	3.8
Goodyear	11.6	9.5	2.1
International Paper	11.0	6.7	4.3
Sears	10.7	7.5	3.2
Union Carbide	9.6	8.5	1.1
American Express	9.5	9.1	0.4
Chevron	8.9	7.8	1.1

that period. If a company is to deliver superior returns to its shareholders, its units must create superior SVA. Calculating superior SVA requires six steps:

- First, develop expectations for the standard drivers of value—sales growth, operating margins, and investments—by factoring in historical performance, the unit's business plan, and competitive benchmarking.

- Second, convert the expectations about value drivers into annual cash-flow estimates and discount them at the business unit's cost of capital in order to obtain the value of each operating unit.

- Third, aggregate the values of each operating unit to verify that the sum is approximately equal to the company's market value.

- Fourth, from the cash flows used to value the operating unit, establish the annual expected SVA over the performance period—typically three years.

- Fifth, use year-end results to compute the actual SVA at the end of each year. The calculation will be the same as in the previous step, with actual numbers replacing the estimates.

- Sixth, calculate the difference between actual and expected SVA. When the difference is positive, you have superior SVA.

Value creation prospects can vary greatly from one business unit to another. An approach based on expectations establishes a level playing field by accounting for differences in business prospects. Managers who perform extraordinarily well in low-return businesses will be rewarded, while those who do poorly in high-return businesses will be penalized. (See the table "The Hierarchy of Performance Measurement.")

At what level of performance do you start rewarding business unit managers with pay for performance? The right answer would seem to be, "When they create superior SVA in their units." But just as they may with indexed options, boards may wish to set their SVA threshold targets at a discount. Setting a threshold that is modestly below expected SVA would be appropriate. Indeed, incentive plans for operating managers often set a threshold at 80% of a designated target. That makes sense, but the converse—imposing a cap—does not. Currently, many plans are capped once performance is greater than 120% of the target. Such a policy would send the wrong message to operating managers who otherwise would be motivated to maximize SVA.

When setting performance pay, it is important to note that value creation is a long-term phenomenon. Annual performance measures do not account for the longer-term consequences of operating and investment decisions made today. So looking at a single year reveals little about the long-term ability of a business to generate cash. To motivate managers to focus on opportunities to create superior SVA beyond the current period, the performance evaluation period should be extended to, say, a rolling three-year cycle. Companies can then retain a portion of incentive payouts to cover against future underperformance.

The Front Line's Contribution

Using SVA performance to establish incentive pay is consistent with the responsibilities of the operating unit

The Hierarchy of Performance Measurement

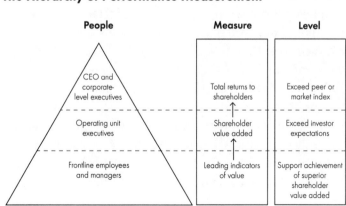

People	Measure	Level
CEO and corporate-level executives	Total returns to shareholders	Exceed peer or market index
Operating unit executives	Shareholder value added	Exceed investor expectations
Frontline employees and managers	Leading indicators of value	Support achievement of superior shareholder value added

executive. But measures are needed at every level of an organization in order for it to realize superior total returns to shareholders. Indeed, finding measures that can guide hands-on decision making by frontline workers is the final piece of the puzzle. Although value drivers such as sales growth and operating margins are useful for identifying value-creating strategies and tracking SVA at operating units, they are not sufficiently focused to provide much day-to-day guidance. Middle managers and frontline employees need to know what specific actions they can take to ensure that expectations are met or exceeded. Even setting a three- or five-year performance period may not capture most of the SVA potential of high-growth businesses or of industries such as pharmaceuticals that have extended lags between their investments and their product sales. The solution to both problems lies in identifying what I call the "leading indicators of value." These indicators can be used both as a supplement to SVA analysis and as the basis for calculating incentives for frontline employees.

Leading indicators are current measures that are strongly correlated with the long-term value of a business. Examples include time to market for new products, employee turnover figures, customer retention rates, the number of new stores that are opened on time, and the average cycle time from order date to shipping date. These are all factors that frontline managers can directly influence. My research has shown that for most businesses, three to six leading indicators account for a high percentage of long-term SVA potential. Improving leading indicators is not a goal in itself; it is the basis for achieving superior SVA. The process of identifying leading indicators is challenging, revealing, and rewarding. It takes more than an impressive knowledge of customers, products, suppliers, and technology to understand a business's sources of value. Operating managers need to identify and focus on activities that maximize SVA and reduce costly investment in resources that contribute little to actual value. Identifying leading indicators helps management find strategies with the highest potential for increasing SVA. "Home Depot's Leading Indicators of Value" at the end of this article shows how one company focuses on certain leading indicators to deliver superior value to shareholders.

Achieving superior returns is the ultimate goal for shareholders. It is, therefore, the only appropriate target for the CEO, the board, and corporate-level executives. Companies with superior performance standards in place at all levels send a powerful message to shareholders about their aspirations.

The focus on achieving superior returns is consistent with the broader duties of the CEO—the responsibility to be in the right businesses and to allocate the proper amount of capital to them. But the most significant source of superior total returns is the operating unit's level of SVA. And the building blocks for SVA are the leading indicators that guide frontline managers. Without performance at those levels, shareholders will not be able to maximize their returns, and CEOs will be less likely to realize gains from their indexed options.

The concept of pay for performance is widely accepted, but the link between incentive pay and superior performance is still too weak. Boards of directors need to push through changes in executive compensation practices, including their own pay schemes. And reforms must be adopted at all levels of the organization.

If indexed options are introduced for CEOs, then SVA-based measures should be introduced in business units. And on the front line, leading indicators should be followed. Shareholders will applaud changes in pay schemes that motivate companies to deliver more value.

Misplaced Concerns About Indexed Options

THE IDEA OF INDEXED OPTIONS is not new. Yet despite their appeal, very few companies have issued them. There are two possible reasons for that. First, current accounting treatment penalizes the use of indexed options; and second, investors may be concerned about the dilution of the value of their shares. Both concerns are largely misplaced.

The Accounting Anomaly

Under present accounting rules, companies must disclose the cost of fixed-price stock options in their financial statements. But they are not required to charge the cost against earnings. In the case of indexed options, however, the difference between the stock price and the exercise price must be reported each year as an expense. It defies economic logic that less costly indexed options must be expensed while more costly standard options are not. But this rule should not be a roadblock against the switch to indexed options. Executive stock options do not become more or less costly depending on whether the disclosure is made in a company's income statement or in its footnotes. Research shows that stock prices respond to disclosure of relevant information such as the cost of executive stock options. Investors are not fooled, and boards should not use the "investors won't understand the earnings hit" excuse to avoid implementing value-creating compensation arrangements.

Still, the requirement to expense indexed options does discourage companies from adopting indexed option plans. Companies do not voluntarily report lower earnings. The Financial Accounting Standards Board should take the lead by mandating a *consistent* treatment for all options. The critical choice for the FASB is not between footnote disclosure and expense recognition. What is important is that whatever the choice, it apply equally to all options. That would level the playing field. Bad accounting policy should not be allowed to dictate compensation.

Fears of Dilution

Shares reserved for outstanding and future grants under stock option and stock purchase programs have surged during the past few years. More than 13% of outstanding shares among the 200 largest public U.S. corporations are reserved for such programs, and some investors believe that allocations have reached—if not exceeded—a reasonable upper limit. Because more indexed options than fixed-price options will have to be granted under the proposed conversion scheme, some shareholders might worry that their holdings will be further diluted.

That is unlikely, because there is a higher chance that indexed options will expire unexercised than is the case with fixed-price options. While indexed options have only about a 50% probability of being exercised (because only about half the companies in an index can enjoy superior performance), fixed-price options have had an exercise rate approaching 100% over the past ten years. Thus if two indexed options were granted in place of each fixed-price option, the increase in a company's outstanding shares would be about the same. Concerns over dilution should not focus on the number of options granted but rather on the number that can be exercised in the absence of superior performance. Because CEOs can be rewarded for weak performance under fixed-price plans, there is actually a greater risk of dilution with standard plans than with indexed plans.

Home Depot's Leading Indicators of Value
Thomas H. Nodine

HOME DEPOT RANKS among the ten largest retailers in the United States. With an annual total return to shareholders of 44.8% over the past ten years, the company's performance easily exceeds the industry average of 21.6%. That extraordinary performance has raised the standards that management must meet in coming years. Over 70% of Home Depot's stock price is based on expected shareholder value added coming from future growth. It is essential that the company identify its leading indicators of value—the building blocks for its long-term SVA—in order to maintain its position.

The first step in finding leading indicators is to see which of the standard cash-flow drivers of value—sales growth, profit margins, and investments—are critical to a company's success. At Home Depot, sales growth and profit margin are the critical drivers. Analyzing sales growth reveals two leading indicators of value—growth in new stores and revenue per store. A sensitivity analysis of those indicators reveals how significantly they are correlated with Home Depot's value. For each 1% shortfall in new store growth, the company's value falls by about 7%. Indeed, store growth is so important to Home Depot that a one-year delay in all currently scheduled new store openings would reduce the company's value by almost 16%.

The same process can be used to identify leading indicators of value associated with profit margins. These include average retail and wholesale prices, as well as freight, labor, and administrative costs as a percentage of revenues.

Understanding the relationship between leading indicators is essential for identifying value-creating strategies. For example, although it is important that Home Depot maintain or exceed projected store growth, the company must not open new stores so quickly that they cannibalize sales at existing stores.

Leading indicators also provide management with a more sophisticated way to identify trends. For example, increases in Home Depot's average retail prices, together with falling average wholesale prices, signal greater future profitability. On the other hand, decreases in Home Depot's revenue per store as growth continues might indicate market saturation, showing managers that a period of lower growth lies ahead.

Home Depot is clearly focusing on leading indicators of value. To promote growth, it is aggressively adding stores in the United States while entering new markets in Canada and Latin America. The retailer is also monitoring store construction to ensure on-time openings, increasing store size to improve revenue per store, and introducing new store formats that promote higher average purchases. At the same time, Home

Depot plans to increase margins by buying in bulk and optimizing its mix of products. By continuing to focus on these leading indicators of value, Home Depot's management can identify value-creating strategies and continue to exceed the high expectations of its shareholders.

Originally published in March–April 1999
Reprint 99210

Why Incentive Plans Cannot Work

ALFIE KOHN

Executive Summary

IT IS DIFFICULT TO overstate the extent to which most managers and the people who advise them believe in the redemptive power of rewards. Certainly, the vast majority of U.S. corporations use some sort of program intended to motivate employees by tying compensation to one index of performance or another. But more striking is the rarely examined belief that people will do a better job if they have been promised some sort of incentive.

This assumption and the practices associated with it are pervasive, but Alfie Kohn examines a growing collection of evidence that supports an opposing view. According to numerous studies in laboratories, workplaces, classrooms, and other settings, rewards typically undermine the very processes they are intended to enhance. The findings suggest that the failure of a given incentive

29

program is due less to a glitch in that program than to the inadequacy of the psychological assumptions that ground all such plans.

Do rewards work? The answer depends on what we mean by "work." Research suggests that, by and large, rewards succeed at securing one thing only: temporary compliance. They do not create an enduring commitment to any value or actions. They merely, and temporarily, change what we do. Kohn explains why rewards fail in a six-point framework: rewards do not motivate; they punish; they rupture relationships; they ignore reasons; they discourage risk taking; and, finally, they undermine interest.

Any manger thinking about a new incentive program—or attached to an old one—would do well to consider Kohn's argument. According to Kohn, incentives (or bribes) simply can't work in the workplace.

IT IS DIFFICULT TO overstate the extent to which most managers and the people who advise them believe in the redemptive power of rewards. Certainly, the vast majority of U.S. corporations use some sort of program intended to motivate employees by tying compensation to one index of performance or another. But more striking is the rarely examined belief that people will do a better job if they have been promised some sort of incentive. This assumption and the practices associated with it are pervasive, but a growing collection of evidence supports an opposing view. According to numerous studies in laboratories,

Most managers too often believe in the redemptive power of rewards.

workplaces, classrooms, and other settings, rewards typically undermine the very processes they are intended to enhance. The findings suggest that the failure of any given incentive program is due less to a glitch in that program than to the inadequacy of the psychological assumptions that ground all such plans.

Temporary Compliance

Behaviorist theory, derived from work with laboratory animals, is indirectly responsible for such programs as piece-work pay for factory workers, stock options for top executives, special privileges accorded to Employees of the Month, and commissions for salespeople. Indeed, the livelihood of innumerable consultants has long been based on devising fresh formulas for computing bonuses to wave in front of

Incentives do not alter the attitudes that underlie our behaviors.

employees. Money, vacations, banquets, plaques—the list of variations on a single, simple behaviorist model of motivation is limitless. And today even many people who are regarded as forward thinking—those who promote teamwork, participative management, continuous improvement, and the like—urge the use of rewards to institute and maintain these very reforms. What we use bribes to accomplish may have changed, but the reliance on bribes, on behaviorist doctrine, has not.

Moreover, the few articles that appear to criticize incentive plans are invariably limited to details of implementation. Only fine-tune the calculations and delivery of the incentive—or perhaps hire the author as a consultant—and the problem will be solved, we are told. As Herbert H. Meyer, professor emeritus in the psychology department at the College of Social and Behavioral Sciences at the University of South Florida, has written, "Anyone reading the literature on this subject published

Rewards do not create a lasting commitment. They merely, and temporarily, change what we do.

20 years ago would find that the articles look almost identical to those published today." That assessment, which could have been written this morning, was

actually offered in 1975. In nearly forty years, the thinking hasn't changed.

Do rewards work? The answer depends on what we mean by "work." Research suggests that, by and large, rewards succeed at securing one thing only: temporary compliance. When it comes to producing lasting change in attitudes and behavior, however, rewards, like punishment, are strikingly ineffective. Once the rewards run out, people revert to their old behaviors. Studies show that offering incentives for losing weight, quitting smoking, using seat belts, or (in the case of children) acting generously is not only less effective than other strategies but often proves worse than doing nothing at all. Incentives, a version of what psychologists call extrinsic motivators, do not alter the attitudes that underlie our behaviors. They do not create an enduring *commitment* to any value or action. Rather, incentives merely—and temporarily—change what we do.

As for productivity, at least two dozen studies over the last three decades have conclusively shown that people who expect to receive a reward for completing a task or for doing that task successfully simply do not perform as well as those who expect no reward at all. These studies examined rewards for children and adults, males and females, and included tasks ranging from memorizing facts to creative problem-solving to designing collages.

In general, the more cognitive sophistication and open-ended thinking that was required, the worse people performed when working for a reward. Interestingly enough, the researchers themselves were often taken by surprise. They assumed that rewards would produce better work but discovered otherwise.

The question for managers is whether incentive plans can work when extrinsic motivators more generally do not. Unfortunately, as author G. Douglas Jenkins, Jr., has noted, most organizational studies to date—like the articles published—have tended "to focus on the effects of *variations* in incentive conditions, and not on whether performance-based pay per se raises performance levels."

A number of studies, however, have examined whether or not pay, especially at the executive level, is related to corporate profitability and other measures of organizational performance. Often they have found slight or even *negative* correlations between pay and performance. Typically, the absence of such a relationship is interpreted as evidence of links between compensation and something other than how well people do their jobs. But most of these data could support a different conclusion, one that reverses the causal arrow. Perhaps what these studies reveal is that higher pay does not produce better performance. In other words, the very idea of trying to reward quality may be a fool's errand.

Consider the findings of Jude T. Rich and John A. Larson, formerly of McKinsey & Company. In 1982, using interviews and proxy statements, they examined compensation programs at 90 major U.S. companies to determine whether return to shareholders was better for corporations that had incentive plans for top executives than it was for those companies that had no such plans. They were unable to find any difference.

Four years later, Jenkins tracked down 28 previously published studies that measured the impact of financial incentives on performance. (Some were conducted in the laboratory and some in the field.) His analysis, "Financial Incentives," published in 1986, revealed that 16, or 57%, of the studies found a positive effect on performance. However, all of the performance measures were quantitative in nature: a good job consisted of producing more of something or doing it faster. Only five of the studies looked at the quality of performance. And none of those five showed any benefits from incentives.

Another analysis took advantage of an unusual situation that affected a group of welders at a Midwestern manufacturing company. At the request of the union, an incentive system that had been in effect for some years was abruptly eliminated. Now, if a financial incentive supplies motivation, its absence should drive down production. And that is exactly what happened, at first. Fortunately, Harold F. Rothe, former personnel manager and corporate staff assistant at the Beloit Corporation, tracked production over a period of months, providing the sort of long-term data rarely collected in this field. After the initial slump, Rothe found that in the absence of incentives the welders' production quickly began to rise and eventually reached a level as high or higher than it had been before.

One of the largest reviews of how intervention programs affect worker productivity, a meta-analysis of some 330 comparisons from 98 studies, was conducted in the mid-1980s by Richard A. Guzzo, associate professor of psychology at the University of Maryland, College Park, and his colleagues at New York University. The raw numbers seemed to suggest a positive relationship between financial incentives and productivity, but because of the huge variations from one study to another, statistical tests indicated that there was no significant effect overall. What's more, financial incentives were virtually unrelated to the number of workers who were absent or who quit their jobs over a period of time. By contrast, training and goal-setting programs had a far greater impact on productivity than did pay-for-performance plans.

Why Rewards Fail

Why do most executives continue to rely on incentive programs? Perhaps it's because few people take the time to examine the connection between incentive programs and problems with workplace productivity and morale. Rewards buy temporary compliance, so it looks like the problems are solved. It's harder to spot the harm they cause over the long term. Moreover, it does not occur to most of us to suspect rewards, given that our own teachers, parents, and managers probably used them. "Do this and you'll get that" is part of the fabric of American life. Finally, by clinging to the belief that motivational problems are due to the particular incentive system in effect at the moment, rather than to the psychological theory behind all incentives, we can remain optimistic that a relatively minor adjustment will repair the damage.

Over the long haul, however, the potential cost to any organization of trying to fine-tune reward-driven compensation systems may be considerable. The fundamental flaws of behaviorism itself doom the prospects of affecting long-term behavior change or performance improvement through the use of rewards. Consider the following six-point framework that examines the true costs of an incentive program.

1. **"Pay is not a motivator."** W. Edward Deming's dec-
laration may seem surprising, even absurd. Of course,
money buys the things people want and need. Moreover,
the less people are paid, the more concerned they are
likely to be about financial matters. Indeed, several studies over the last few decades have found that when people are asked to guess what matters to their coworkers—
or, in the case of managers, to their subordinates—they
assume money heads the list. But put the question
directly—"What do you care about?"—and pay typically
ranks only fifth or sixth.

Even if people were principally concerned with their
salaries, this does not prove that money is motivating.
There is no firm basis for the assumption that paying
people more will encourage them to do better work or
even, in the long run, more work. As Frederick Herzberg,
Distinguished Professor
of Management at the
University of Utah's Graduate School of Manage-
ment, has argued, just
because too little money
can irritate and demoti-

*Punishment and rewards
are actually two sides of the
same coin. Both have a
punitive effect because they
are manipulative.*

vate does not mean that more and more money will
bring about increased satisfaction, much less increased
motivation. It is plausible to assume that if someone's
take-home pay was cut in half, his or her morale would
suffer enough to undermine performance. But it doesn't
necessarily follow that doubling that person's pay would
result in better work.

2. **Rewards punish.** Many managers understand that
coercion and fear destroy motivation and create defi-
ance, defensiveness, and rage. They realize that punitive
management is a contradiction in terms. As Herzberg

wrote in HBR some 25 years ago ("One More Time: How Do You Motivate Employees?" January–February 1968), a "KITA"—which, he coyly explains, stands for "kick in the pants"—may produce movement but never motivation.

What most executives fail to recognize is that Herzberg's observation is equally true of rewards. Punishment and rewards are two sides of the same coin. Rewards have a punitive effect because they, like outright punishment, are manipulative. "Do this and you'll get that" is not really very different from "Do this or here's what will happen to you." In the case of incentives, the reward itself may be highly desired; but by making that bonus contingent on certain behaviors, managers manipulate their subordinates, and that experience of being controlled is likely to assume a punitive quality over time.

Further, not receiving a reward one had expected to receive is also indistinguishable from being punished. Whether the incentive is witheld or withdrawn deliberately, or simply not received by someone who had hoped to get it, the effect is identical. And the more desirable the reward, the more demoralizing it is to miss out.

The new school, which exhorts us to catch people doing something right and reward them for it, is not very different from the old school, which advised us to catch people doing something wrong and threaten to punish them if they ever do it again. What is essentially taking place in both approaches is that a lot of people are getting caught. Managers are creating a workplace in which people feel controlled, not an environment conducive to exploration, learning, and progress.

3. Rewards rupture relationships. Relationships among employees are often casualties of the scramble for rewards. As leaders of the Total Quality Management movement have emphasized, incentive programs, and the performance appraisal systems that accompany them, reduce the possibilities for cooperation. Peter R. Scholtes, senior management consultant at Joiner Associates Inc., put it starkly, "Everyone is pressuring the system for individual gain. No one is improving the system for collective gain. The system will inevitably crash." Without teamwork, in other words, there can be no quality.

The surest way to destroy cooperation and, therefore, organizational excellence, is to force people to compete for rewards or recognition or to rank them against each other. For each person who wins, there are many others who carry with them the feeling of having lost. And the more these awards are publicized through the use of memos, newsletters, and awards banquets, the more detrimental their impact can be. Furthermore, when employees compete for a limited number of incentives, they will most likely begin to see each other as obstacles to their own success. But the same result can occur with any use of rewards; introducing competition just makes a bad thing worse.

Relationships between supervisors and subordinates can also collapse under the weight of incentives. Of course, the supervisor who punishes is about as welcome to employees as a glimpse of a police car in their rearview mirrors. But even the supervisor who rewards can produce some damaging reactions. For instance, employees may be tempted to conceal any problems they might be having and present themselves as infinitely competent to the manager in control of the money. Rather than ask for help—a prerequisite for optimal performance—they might opt instead for flattery, attempting to convince the manager that they have everything under control. Very few things threaten an organization as much as a hoard of incentive-driven individuals trying to curry favor with the incentive dispenser.

4. Rewards ignore reasons. In order to solve problems in the workplace, managers must understand what caused them. Are employees inadequately prepared for the demands of their jobs? Is long-term growth being sacrificed to maximize short-term return? Are workers unable to collaborate effectively? Is the organization so rigidly hierarchical that employees are intimidated about making recommendations and feel powerless and burned out? Each of these situations calls for a different response. But relying on incentives to boost productivity does nothing to address possible underlying problems and bring about meaningful change.

Moreover, managers often use incentive systems as a substitute for giving workers what they need to do a good job. Treating workers well—providing useful feedback, social support, and the room for self-determination—is the essence of good management. On the other hand, dangling a bonus in front of employees and waiting for the results requires much less effort. Indeed, some evidence suggests that productive managerial strategies are less

The number one casualty of rewards is creativity. As the late John Condry put it, rewards are the "enemies of exploration."

likely to be used in organizations that lean on pay-for-performance plans. In his study of welders' performance, Rothe noted that supervisors tended to "demonstrate relatively less leadership" when incentives were in place. Likewise, author Carla O'Dell reports in *People, Performance, and Pay* that a survey of 1,600 organizations by the American Productivity Center discovered little in the way of active employee involvement in organizations that used small-group incentive plans. As Jone L. Pearce, associate professor at the Graduate School of Management, University of California at Irvine, wrote in "Why Merit Pay Doesn't Work: Implications from Organization Theory," pay for performance actually "impedes the ability of managers to manage."

5. Rewards discourage risk-taking. "People will do precisely what they are asked to do if the reward is significant," enthused Monroe J. Haegele, a proponent of pay-for-performance programs, in "The New Performance Measures." And here is the root of the problem. Whenever people are encouraged to think about what they will get for engaging in a task, they become less inclined to take risks or explore possibilities, to play hunches or to consider incidental stimuli. In a word, the number one casualty of rewards is creativity.

Excellence pulls in one direction; rewards pull in another. Tell people that their income will depend on their productivity or performance rating, and they will focus on the numbers. Sometimes they will manipulate the schedule for completing tasks or even engage in patently unethical and illegal behavior. As Thane S. Pittman, professor and chair of the psychology department at Gettysburg College, and his colleagues point out, when we are motivated by incentives, "features such as predictability and simplicity are desirable, since the primary focus associated with this orientation is to get through the task expediently in order to reach the desired goal."

Do rewards motivate people? Absolutely. They motivate people to get rewards.

The late Cornell University professor, John Condry, was more succinct: rewards, he said, are the "enemies of exploration."

Consider the findings of organizational psychologist Edwin A. Locke. When Locke paid subjects on a piece-rate basis for their work, he noticed that they tended to choose easier tasks as the payment for success increased. A number of other studies have also found that people working for a reward generally try to minimize challenge. It isn't that human beings are naturally lazy or that it is unwise to give employees a voice in determining the standards to be used. Rather, people tend to lower their sights when they are encouraged to think about what they are going to get for their efforts. "Do this and you'll get that," in other words, focuses attention on the "that" instead of the "this." Emphasizing large bonuses is the last strategy we should use if we care about innovation. Do rewards motivate people? Absolutely. They motivate people to get rewards.

6. Rewards undermine interest. If our goal is excellence, no artificial incentive can ever match the power of intrinsic motivation. People who do exceptional work may be glad to be paid and even more glad to be well paid, but they do not work to collect a paycheck. They work because they love what they do.

Few will be shocked by the news that extrinsic motivators are a poor substitute for genuine interest in one's job. What is far more surprising is that rewards, like punishment, may actually undermine the intrinsic motivation that results in optimal performance. The more a manager stresses what an employee can earn for good work, the less interested that employee will be in the work itself.

The first studies to establish the effect of rewards on intrinsic motivation were conducted in the early 1970s by Edward Deci, professor and chairman of the psychology department at the University of Rochester. By now, scores of experiments across the country have replicated the finding. As Deci and his colleague Richard Ryan, senior vice president of investment and training manager at Robert W. Baird and Co., Inc., wrote in their 1985 book, *Intrinsic Motivation and Self-Determination in Human Behavior*, "the research has consistently shown that any contingent payment system tends to undermine intrinsic motivation." The basic effect is the same for a variety of rewards and tasks, although extrinsic motivators are particularly destructive when tied to interesting or complicated tasks.

Deci and Ryan argue that receiving a reward for a particular behavior sends a certain message about what we have done and controls, or attempts to control, our future behavior. The more we experience being controlled, the more we will tend to lose interest in what we are doing. If we go to work thinking about the possibility of getting a bonus, we come to feel that our work is not self-directed. Rather, it is the reward that drives our behavior.

Other theorists favor a more simple explanation for the negative effect rewards have on intrinsic motivation: anything presented as a prerequisite for something else—that is, as a means toward another end—comes to be seen as less desirable. The recipient of the reward assumes, "If they have to bribe me to do it, it must be something I wouldn't want to do." In fact, a series of studies, published in 1992 by psychology professor Jonathan L. Freedman and his colleagues at the University of Toronto, confirmed that the larger the incentive we are offered, the more negatively we will view the activity for which the bonus was received. (The activities themselves don't seem to matter; in this study, they ranged from participating in a medical experiment to eating unfamiliar food.) Whatever the reason for the effect, however, any incentive or pay-for-performance system tends to make people less enthusiastic about their work and therefore less likely to approach it with a commitment to excellence.

Dangerous Assumptions

Outside of psychology departments, few people distinguish between intrinsic and extrinsic motivation. Those who do assume that the two concepts can simply be added together for best effect. Motivation comes in two flavors, the logic goes, and both together must be better than either alone. But studies show that the real world works differently.

Some managers insist that the only problem with incentive programs is that they don't reward the right things. But these managers fail to understand the psychological factors involved and, consequently, the risks of sticking with the status quo.

Contrary to conventional wisdom, the use of rewards is not a response to the extrinsic orientation exhibited by many workers. Rather, incentives help create this focus on financial considerations. When an organization uses a Skinnerian management or compensation system, people are likely to become less interested in their work, requiring extrinsic incentives before expending effort. Then supervisors shake their heads and say, "You see? If you don't offer them a reward, they won't do anything." It is a classic self-fulfilling prophecy. Swarthmore College psychology professor Barry Schwartz has conceded that behavior theory may seem to provide us with a useful way of describing what goes on in U.S. workplaces. However, "It does this not because work is a natural exemplification of behavior theory principles but because behavior theory principles . . . had a significant hand in transforming work into an exemplification of behavior theory principles."

Managers who insist that the job won't get done right without rewards have failed to offer a convincing argument for behavioral manipulation. Promising a reward to someone who appears unmotivated is a bit like offering salt water to someone who is thirsty. Bribes in the workplace simply can't work.

On Incentives

"The Pay-for-Performance Dilemma"
by Herbert H. Meyer
Organizational Dynamics
Winter 1975.

"Financial Incentives"
by G. Douglas Jenkins, Jr.
in *Generalizing from Laboratory to Field Settings*
edited by Edwin A. Locke
Lexington, MA: Lexington Books, 1986.

"Why Some Long-Term Incentives Fail"
by Jude T. Rich and John A. Larson
in *Incentives, Cooperation, and Risk Sharing*
edited by Haig R. Nalbantian
Totowa, NJ: Rowman & Littlefield, 1987.

**"Output Rates Among Welders:
Productivity and Consistency
Following Removal of a Financial
Incentive System"**
by Harold F. Rothe
Journal of Applied Psychology
December 1970.

**"The Effects of Psychologically
Based Intervention Programs on
Worker Productivity: A Meta-Analysis"**
by Richard A. Guzzo, Richard D. Jette,
and Raymond A. Katzell
Personnel Psychology
Summer 1985.

**"One More Time: How Do You
Motivate Employees?"**
by Frederick Herzberg
Harvard Business Review
January–February 1968.

**"An Elaboration on Deming's
Teachings on Performance Appraisal"**
by Peter R. Scholtes
in *Performance Appraisal:
Perspectives on a Quality
Management Approach*
edited by Gary N. McLean, et al.
Alexandria, VA: University of
Minnesota Training and
Development Research Center and
American Society for Training and
Development, 1990.

People, Performance, and Pay
by Carla O'Dell

Houston: American Productivity
Center, 1987.

**"Why Merit Pay Doesn't Work:
Implications from Organization Theory"**
by Jone L. Pearce in *New Perspectives
on Compensation*
edited by David B. Balkin and
Luis R. Gomez-Mejia
Englewood Cliffs, NJ:
Prentice-Hall, 1987.

"The New Performance Measures"
by Monroe J. Haegele
in *The Compensation Handbook*
Third Edition
edited by Milton L. Rock and
Lance A. Berger
New York: McGraw-Hill, 1991.

**"Intrinsic and Extrinsic
Motivational Orientations: Reward-Induced
Changes in Preference for Complexity"**
by Thane S. Pittman, Jolee Emery,
and Ann K. Boggiano
Journal of Personality and Social Psychology
March 1982.

**"Enemies of Exploration: Self-Initiated
Versus Other-Initiated Learning"**
by John Condry
Journal of Personality and Social Psychology
July 1977.

**"Toward a Theory of Task
Motivation and Incentives"**
by Edwin A. Locke
Organizational Behavior and

Human Performance
Volume 3, 1968.

**Intrinsic Motivation and Self-
Determination in Human Behavior**
by Edward L. Deci and
Richard M. Ryan
New York: Plenum Press, 1985.

**"Inferred Values and the
Reverse-Incentive Effect in
Induced Compliance"**
by Jonathan L. Freedman, John A.
Cunningham, and Kirsten Krismer
*Journal of Personality and
Social Psychology*
March 1992.

**The Battle for Human Nature:
Science, Morality and Modern Life**
by Barry Schwartz
New York: W.W. Norton and
Company, 1986.

Recommended Reading

**"A Model of Creativity and
Innovation in Organizations"**
by Teresa M. Amabile
in *Research in Organizational
Behavior,* Volume 10
edited by Barry M. Staw and
L.L. Cummings
Greenwich, CT: JAI Press, Inc., 1988.

Out of the Crisis
by W. Edwards Deming
Cambridge, MA: MIT Center for
Advanced Engineering Study, 1986.

"Merit Pay, Performance Targeting, and Productivity"
by Arie Halachmi and Marc Holzer
Review of Public Personnel Administration
Spring 1987.

No Contest: The Case Against Competition, Revised Edition
by Alfie Kohn
Boston: Houghton Mifflin, 1992.

Punished by Rewards: The Trouble with Gold Stars, Incentive Plans, A's, Praise, and Other Bribes
by Alfie Kohn
Boston: Houghton Mifflin, 1993.

The Market Experience
by Robert E. Lane
Cambridge, England:
Cambridge University Press, 1991.

The Hidden Costs of Reward: New Perspectives on the Psychology of Human Motivation
edited by Mark R. Lepper and
David Greene
Hillsdale, NJ: L. Erlbaum
Associates, 1978.

The Great Jackass Fallacy
by Harry Levinson

Cambridge, MA: Harvard University
Press, 1973.

The Human Side of Enterprise
by Douglas McGregor
New York: McGraw-Hill, 1960.

Wealth Addiction
by Philip Slater
New York: Dutton, 1980.

**Money and Motivation: An
Analysis of Incentives in Industry**
by William Foote Whyte and
Melville Dalton, et al.
New York: Harper, 1955.

Originally published in September–October 1993
Reprint 93506

Rethinking Rewards

ALFIE KOHN

Executive Summary

IT IS DIFFICULT TO overstate the extent to which most managers and the people who advise them believe in the redemptive power of rewards, argues Alfie Kohn in "Why Incentive Plans Cannot Work" (Chapter 2). The assumption that people will do a better job if they are promised an incentive is pervasive, but a growing collection of evidence supports an opposing view. In fact, research suggests that, by and large, rewards succeed at securing one thing only: temporary compliance. According to Kohn, incentives—or bribes—simply can't work.

Kohn's views elicited a lively debate on the role of incentives in the workplace. In this chapter, nine experts consider Kohn's argument. Kohn then offers a general response. Some experts:

"A world without A's, praise, gold stars, or incentives? No thank you, Mr. Kohn. Communism was tried, and it didn't work."
—G. BENNETT STEWART III

"The problem is not that incentives can't work but that they work all too well."
—GEORGE P. BAKER III

"Incentives are neither all good nor all bad. Although not the right answer in all cases, they can be highly effective motivational tools and should be employed under the appropriate circumstances."
—DONITA S. WOLTERS

"It would be a mistake to believe that reward and recognition must always have a negative effect on performance or that creative people cannot be motivated by both money and interest in the work itself."
—TERESA M. AMABILE

It is difficult to overstate the extent to which most managers—and the people who advise them—believe in the redemptive power of rewards, Alfie Kohn argues in "Why Incentive Plans Cannot Work" (chapter 2). Certainly, the vast majority of U.S. corporations use some sort of program intended to motivate employees by tying compensation to one index of performance or another. But more striking is the rarely examined belief that people will do a better job if they have been promised some sort of incentive.

This assumption and the practices associated with it are pervasive, but a growing collection of evidence supports an opposing view. According to numerous studies in laboratories, workplaces, classrooms, and other settings, rewards typically undermine the very processes they are intended to enhance. In Kohn's view, the findings suggest that the failure of any given incentive program is due less to a glitch in that program than to the inadequacy of the psychological assumptions that ground all such plans.

Do rewards work? The answer depends on what we mean by "work." Research suggests that, by and large, rewards succeed at securing one thing only: temporary compliance. They do not create an enduring commitment to any value or action. They merely, and temporarily, change what we do. According to Kohn, incentives in the workplace simply can't work.

Nine experts consider the role of rewards in the workplace.

G. BENNETT STEWART III
Senior Partner, Stern Stewart & Co., New York, New York

A WORLD WITHOUT A's, praise, gold stars, or incentives? No thank you, Mr. Kohn. Communism was tried, and it didn't work.

The Soviet and Chinese economies collapsed because people were not allowed to share in the fruits of their individual efforts. With gains from personal initiative harvested as a public good, innovation ceased, and productivity froze. "They pretend to pay us, and we pretend to work" was the Russian worker's lament for the system Kohn now proposes. But for pay to mean anything, it must be linked to performance. Without that link, pay becomes nothing more than entitlement, a job nothing more than a sinecure.

"A world without A's, praise, gold stars, or incentives? No thank you, Mr. Kohn. Communism was tried, and it didn't work."

—G. Bennett Stewart III

Kohn is unhappy that rewarding some people necessitates penalizing others. Winston Churchill's apt aphorism is the best response. He said, "The virtue of communism is the equal sharing of its misery, and the vice of capitalism is the unequal sharing of its blessings." You can't have it both ways, Mr. Kohn. You simply can't have the equality of outcome you desire with the robust, dynamic economy we all want.

Contrary to the small-sample psychology tests Kohn cites, the responsiveness of ordinary citizens to incentives is demonstrated daily in our economy. Consumers cut consumption in reaction to the "penalty" of a price increase and raise purchases in reaction to the "bribe" of a lower price. The price system efficiently allocates scarce resources precisely because it rewards people who conserve and penalizes those who fail to respond. Can it be true, as Kohn seems to think, that people respond to monetary incentives when they *spend* their income but not when they *earn* it?

If Kohn makes a useful point, it is when he says that people won't want to be paid for doing specific tasks. But here is where we disagree: people should be rewarded for an overall job done well. To put the point in economic terms, the best incentive is having a piece of the action. Company stock, however, is not the best approach to instilling ownership, for it frequently leaves too loose a link between pay and performance.

The best approach often is to carve employees into a share of the profit contributed by their part of the company. Profit should be defined in relevant cash-flow terms after covering the cost of all capital employed, a measure that Stern Stewart & Co. calls Economic Value Added. EVA provides employees with three clear incentives: to improve profitability, to grow profitability, and to withdraw resources from uneconomic activities. In addition, it ties their decisions and energies directly to the "net present value" of their enterprise. All key managers at Quaker Oats have been on an EVA sharing plan for several years, and Scott Paper Company introduced an EVA incentive program for all salaried employees at the beginning of 1993, to name but 2 of the 50 prominent companies that have adopted this approach in recent years.

EILEEN APPELBAUM
Associate Research Director, Economic Policy Institute, Washington, D.C.

COMPANIES TODAY are under intense pressure to improve efficiency and quality at a time when their resources are severely limited. Fiddling with compensation schemes appeals to many managers as a cheap way to improve their companies' performance by providing individuals with incentives to work harder. In fact, reliance on individual incentives to motivate workers and spur productivity has a long history in the United States. The U.S. human-resource model evolved in the 1950s partly in response to then-current theories of industrial psychology. By designing compensation schemes that recognize and reward individual differences, companies expected to reap the rewards of increased employee motivation and improved job performance. This idea continues to inform present managerial thinking. In "Why Incentive Plans Cannot Work," Alfie Kohn has performed an important service by marshaling the modern evidence on the psychological effects of incentives and by showing that rewards fail to improve, and may even reduce, performance.

We are still left, however, with questions about what improves a company's performance and what role compensation actually plays in that improvement. I would offer the following answers, based on an analysis of nearly 200 academic case studies and consultants' reports, carried out with Rosemary Batt—a doctoral candidate in labor relations and human-resource policy at MIT's Sloan School of Management—and published in *The New American Workplace,* forthcoming from the ILR Press in 1994.

In the early part of the twentieth century, workplace innovations attempted to improve employee satisfaction and, at the same time, company performance. In contrast, the move to high-performance work systems since the mid-1980s is motivated by the need to improve quality and reduce costs simultaneously. In the mass-production model of work organization, whether the Taylorist or the U.S. HR version, improving quality raises costs—for inspection, supervision, rework, and waste. It was quite a shock to U.S. sensibilities, therefore, when Japanese auto manufacturers demonstrated that new ways of organizing work could deliver noticeably higher quality and customer satisfaction at significantly lower prices. It took nearly a decade for companies in the United States to realize that they would have to change.

Our review of the evidence indicates an acceleration of experimentation with innovative workplace practices and the emergence since the mid-1980s of two distinctly *American* high-performance models: a U.S. version of lean production that relies on employee involvement and a U.S. version of team production that relies on employee empowerment for performance gains. Productivity and performance improve the most when work is reorganized so that employees have the training, opportunity, and authority to participate effectively in decision making; when they have assurances that they will not be punished for expressing unpopular ideas; when they realize that they will not lose their jobs as a result of contributing their knowledge to improve productivity; and when they know that they will receive a fair share of any performance gains, assurances which unionized workers in high-performance companies enjoy.

Attempts to improve performance by manipulating compensation packages have proven counterproductive. However, reorganizing the work process to capitalize on employee skills and participation has improved performance, especially in combination with employment security, gainsharing, and incentives to take part in training. In this sense, then, compensation packages are an important component of the human-resource practices that are necessary to support high-performance work systems.

MICHAEL BEER
Professor of Business Administration, Harvard Business School, Boston, Massachusetts

KOHN HAS MOUNTED an eloquent argument, when it is considered in light of what we know about motivation and organizational effectiveness. But because certain practical considerations and cultural differences are not addressed, the argument is flawed.

Like Kohn, I have found that many managers in the United States and the United Kingdom—but not, incidentally, in continental Europe or Japan—have deeply held assumptions about the role of incentive pay in motivation. These assumptions lead them to engage compensation consultants in answering the wrong question: How should we design the incentive system in order to obtain the desired behavior? The more important question is: What role, if any, should incentive compensation play? Like Kohn, I have found that assumptions about incentive compensation have led many managers to expect incentives to solve organizational problems, when there are actually deeper underlying reasons for those problems.

"If incentive systems do not motivate, what should managers do about compensation? Surely, Kohn would not suggest that everyone be paid the same."
—Michael Beer

Managers tend to use compensation as a crutch. After all, it is far easier to design an incentive system that will do management's work than it is to articulate a direction persuasively, develop agreement about goals and problems, and confront difficulties when they arise. The half-life of an incentive system is at best five years. When it stops paying off, employees turn against it. And the result is another dysfunctional by-product of incentive systems: precious attention, time, and money is expended on endless debates about and redesigns of the incentive system.

If incentive systems do not motivate, what should managers do about compensation? Surely, Kohn would not suggest that everyone should be paid the same. In some industries or functions—sales, for example— incentive compensation is the prevailing practice. In these areas, without paying for performance, an organization will lose its best people. Yet by paying for performance, the company runs the danger of encouraging self-interest instead of organizational commitment. This is a fundamental pay-for-performance dilemma that practicing managers confront and that Kohn neglects to address.

It is undoubtedly true that in today's competitive environment, interdependence between different business units and functions as well as the need for customer service and quality make incentive compensation less appropriate than it once was. But there are circumstances in which it is the only solution available: for example, managers of independent stores far from headquarters who don't have a motivating manager-subordinate relationship or salespeople whose performance is independent of other business units and who operate without supervision much of the time.

Managers who agree with Kohn should pay for performance but strive to use incentive systems as little as possible. Pay is an exercise in smoke and mirrors. Companies cannot stop paying for performance. However, they should avoid using incentives for all the reasons that Kohn suggests.

What can managers do? They should focus on paying people equitably, rather than using pay as an instrument of motivation. They should avoid coupling pay with yearly or quarterly performance, while promoting the top 10% or 15% of employees for outstanding long-term contributions. The poorest performers should be weeded out, while the rest should be praised for good performance and recognized through other means to promote self-esteem.

We are indebted to Kohn for ringing the alarm, but he does not provide managers with creative, practical solutions to the pay-for-performance dilemma.

ANDREW M. LEBBY
Senior Partner, The Performance Group, Washington, D.C.

THE EFFECT OF REWARDS on motivation and performance is one of the most studied subjects in the management literature. Year after year we validate the finding that employees' perceptions of underpay result in decreased productivity, while increased pay doesn't result in increased productivity. Year after year we ask employees what motivates them, and year after year they reply: a sense of accomplishment in performing the work itself, recognition from peers and top management, career advancement, management support, and, only then, salary.

If Kohn is unable to find data that support anything but a negative relationship between financial incentives and performance, why is it that in the face of overwhelming evidence executives continue to hold onto ineffective methods? Why is it that they refuse to provide those things that employees say they want, that directly relate to increased productivity, and that have little or no financial cost?

When we stop to separate the physical nature of the reward itself from what the recipient finds rewarding, some possible answers appear. When we ask employees, "What was the last reward you received?" the most frequent response is some variant of "money." When we ask, "What did you find rewarding about money?" the most frequent response is that it was a tacit acknowledgment of the outstanding nature of their contribution. Just as it is easier for some parents to show love with gifts than with hugs, it is often easier for organizations and managers to show gratitude with money than with words.

Our current notions of pay follow naturally from our antiquated, Taylorist, mechanistic models for designing work. The work we do and how we do it have shifted significantly, but our reward and salary structures remain essentially the same. Senior managers will end financial incentives only when they rethink what work is and how it is performed. Organizations that have redesigned work to reflect cross-functional business processes or those that have implemented the actual *principles* of TQM have had to rethink pay and performance. Employees have said, "Give us the tools, the skills, the information, the support, and the respect we need." In different words, "Give us real capital, intellectual capital, and symbolic capital, and we'll increase your—and our—financial capital."

Money is an outcome of high performance. Satisfaction and respect are incentives to it.

TERESA M. AMABILE
Professor of Psychology, Brandeis University, Waltham, Massachusetts

KOHN IS ABSOLUTELY RIGHT when he tells us that rewards can work against real commitment and creativity. But he doesn't tell the whole story. There are important differences between bribes and equitable compensation, and there are conditions under which rewards can *increase* involvement and creativity. What matters is what those rewards actually mean.

As Kohn points out, there is abundant evidence that interest and performance decline over the long run when people feel they are controlled by incentive systems or any other management system. What Kohn fails to point out is that people do not always feel controlled by rewards. In a recent study of professional artists, my students and I found, as Kohn would have predicted, that noncommissioned works were more creative than commissioned works. However, what mattered was not the obvious fact of contracting for reward, but the degree to which the artist felt constrained by the terms of the commission: the more constraints, the lower the creativity. In fact, some artists considered some of their commissions enabling, allowing them to create an interesting work of art that they wouldn't otherwise have had the means to do. When the reward presented the artist with new possibilities, in other words, creativity actually increased.

> *"Intrinsic motivation—being motivated by challenge and enjoyment—is essential to creativity. But extrinsic motivation—being motivated by recognition and money—doesn't necessarily hurt."*
> —Teresa M. Amabile

Intrinsic motivation—being motivated by challenge and enjoyment—is essential to creativity. But extrinsic motivation—being motivated by recognition and money—doesn't necessarily hurt. The most creative artists in our study tended to be motivated more by challenge, but they also tended to be motivated by recognition. Kohn accurately documents the evidence that rewards can undermine creativity. But he fails to mention the evidence that tangible rewards can actually enhance creativity under certain circumstances, most notably when the individual's primary focus is on the intrinsic reward of the work itself.

Bribes, as Kohn frequently notes, are bound to make people feel controlled, and he rightly points out their negative effect on people's work. But he implicitly includes salary in the same category as bribes when he argues that "pay is not a motivator." Certainly, there are some circumstances under which salary increases are perceived as bribes. A few years ago, for example, I interviewed an R&D scientist who was widely considered to be one of the three most important innovators in a large, successful company; he was also considered extremely eccentric. "They offered me a pretty large salary increase this year, but I refused it," he recounted. "Right now, my lab is my playground; I pretty much come in here and do things the way I want. But the more they pay you, the more they think they own you."

A much more common reaction, however, was the feeling expressed by other scientists that their salary increases recognized their creative contributions. Generous compensation, including companywide profit sharing, need not be seen as a bribe, particularly when it is presented as the equitable outcome of creative competence.

Although Kohn's article is clear about what managers should avoid, it has little to say about alternatives to incentives. There is much that can be said about redesigning work and the work environment so that extrinsic motivators become less central. Managers need to know how to use these alternative techniques before they can be expected to abandon the incentive systems on which they have relied for so long.

If Kohn can convince even a few managers that incentive plans are not the keys to innovative, high-quality performance, he will have made a significant contribution. But it would be a mistake to believe that reward and recognition must always have a negative effect on performance or that creative people cannot be motivated by both money and interest in the work itself. As the poet Anne Sexton once said, "I am in love with money, so don't be mistaken. But first I want to write good poems. After that, I am anxious as hell to earn money and fame and bring the stars all down."

JERRY MCADAMS
Vice President, Performance Improvement Resources, Maritz Inc., Director, Consortium for Alternative Reward Strategies Research, St. Louis, Missouri

A FEW YEARS AGO, Kohn did the business community a service with his book, *No Contest: The Case Against Competition,* which argues that competition is for the *marketplace* rather than the *workplace.* The book makes a compelling argument for focusing on team work instead of pitting one employee against another. The key to success, Kohn maintains, is to create an atmosphere of cooperation, channeling employees' creativity and energy to affect the business objectives of the organization positively. Competition between individuals, on the other hand, only gets in the way.

> "Appropriate rewards for improved performance have always made good sense, intuitively and practically. They aren't wrong. They aren't intrinsically demotivating."
> —Jerry McAdams

Now Kohn argues that rewards get in the way as well. On the basis of my 20 years of researching and designing reward plans for sales and nonsales employees, I disagree. Appropriate rewards for improved performance have always made good sense, intuitively and practically. They aren't wrong. They aren't intrinsically demotivating. Data show they make good business sense.

Of course, there is always a market for speeches, books, and articles that profess, through highly selective academic research, that what *is* working really *isn't*. Kohn's article is a provocative exercise in attention-getting, niche marketing. Unfortunately, Kohn's article will probably be used by some to deny performance-improvement opportunities.

I do agree with Kohn's point regarding the negative aspects of the reinforcement of tasks, particularly when the reinforcement plan is piece-rate or merit-pay based. Measuring and rewarding on an individual level (sales excepted) does tend to become controlling. The focus should be on business objectives, not tasks. The study, *Capitalizing on Human Assets*, covering one-million employees and 432 compensation plans and sponsored by the nonprofit Consortium for Alternative Reward Strategies Research (CARS), shows that rewarding groups of employees, usually whole plants and offices, is a powerful business strategy. According to the study, this strategy pays off a median three-to-one return on the cost of the rewards. Employees earn from 2% to 15% of their base pay in incentives or noncash awards. No layoffs appear to result from the improved performance. Interviews and extensive data analysis of the 432 plans show positive employee-management cooperation and improved information sharing and employee involvement.

Rewards are not bribes. Bribes are payments for behavior that may be in the organization's best interest but are clearly *not* in the individual's. Rewards reinforce a "win-win" environment. The objective of a reward plan is not to "control or manipulate," as Kohn contends. It is to provide focus and reward improved performance.

Tom Peters was right when he wrote about Kohn's thesis, "What we need is a lot *more* positive reinforcement, and a lot less of the negative kind, throughout the corporate landscape. And far from cautioning companies about the dangers of incentives, we should be applauding those that offer their employees a bigger piece of the action" (INC, April 1988). The CARS research has done just that, looking at more plans in greater depth than any other study. The bottom line is simple: reward plans work when properly designed and supported; there can be something in it for everyone.

"I'll accept that elephants cannot fly and that fish cannot walk, but Kohn's argument that incentive plans cannot work defies the laws of nature at Tyco Laboratories."
—*L. Dennis Kozlowski*

I think it is time to focus on the productive use of people as assets to business not on the counterproductive theories in Kohn's article.

L. DENNIS KOZLOWSKI
Chairman and CEO, Tyco Laboratories, Inc., Exeter, New Hampshire

I'LL ACCEPT THAT elephants cannot fly and that fish cannot walk, but Kohn's argument that incentive plans cannot work defies the laws of nature at Tyco Laboratories. Tyco provides a compelling case study that incentives *can* and *do* work for both managers and shareholders. In fact, we believe our incentive compensation program is at the heart of our company's success.

We view the relationship between Tyco's management and its shareholders as very straightforward: management works for the shareholders. It is our mission to create value for them through stock-price appreciation. In fact, our share price has closely tracked our earnings curve for many years, lending considerable weight to our determination to encourage earnings growth in a prudent and consistent manner. Our compensation program, in turn, was designed to align the financial interests of our executives with those of our shareholders. The basic rule is this: the more the executives earn for the shareholders, the more they earn for themselves.

Tyco's 250 profit centers fall into four major businesses. Within the context of a few corporate financial controls, we tell each profit-center manager to run the business as if he or she owned it. A decentralized approach lets us put the financial resources of a $3-billion corporation behind the entrepreneurial spirit, drive, and resourcefulness of managers who think and act like owners. It's the best of both worlds. Profit-center autonomy and responsibility go hand in hand. We encourage each unit's management team to share the unit's profits. The more profits the business unit earns for the shareholders, the more compensation the management team earns for itself.

Our incentive plan has several important and unique features. For one, incentive compensation is directly tied to each business unit's performance and not to corporate results or other factors beyond any individual's control. In addition, the awards are not based on how units perform against a budget or any other preset goal. Instead, awards constitute a preestablished percentage of earnings. Since we adopted this approach, the quality of the budgeting process has substantially improved. Finally, award opportunities are uncapped, and, as a result, they encourage the entrepreneurial spirit that we value.

When designed effectively and integrated thoroughly into the management process, executive incentive programs work well for management and shareholders alike.

GEORGE P. BAKER III
Associate Professor, Harvard Business School,
Boston, Massachusetts

THE PROBLEM IS NOT that incentives can't work but that they work all too well. Kohn's analysis of the unintended and unwanted side effects of many incentive plans is perfectly apt; plans that provide incentives for the wrong behavior will produce the wrong results. However, Kohn's solution to abandon incentive plans entirely is misguided. Rather, managers must learn how to harness and use the power of incentives to drive individual motivation and organizational effectiveness.

In several places, Kohn's assertions about the weakness of incentive plans only serve to highlight the power of such plans to influence behavior. What Kohn says is absolutely true: if teamwork and cooperation are desired, and the incentive plan rewards only individual results, then the plan will generate counterproductive results. However, a well-designed incentive plan that rewards team productivity not only will avoid such unproductive behavior but also will induce employee cooperation. This is the logical basis for the majority of profit-sharing and employee stock-ownership plans, whose effectiveness mounting evidence supports.

Similarly, Kohn's observation that incentive plans cause employees to curry favor with the boss and withhold information about poor performance is often accurate. But the solution is not to eliminate the boss's ability to reward employees. Instead, supervisors should be trained to ignore or punish politicking. It is precisely because incentives are so powerful that Kohn can predict that if managers reward politicking, politicking will result.

Reward plans need not be controlling, as Kohn seems to imply. Consider the store-manager incentive plan at Au Bon Pain. Store managers are given a profitability target and are allowed to keep a substantial fraction of any profits they earn above this target. The chain puts few constraints on how they achieve or exceed their targets. The plan has hardly been "the enemy of exploration." Rather, it has resulted in an explosion of entrepreneurial experimentation and innovation. Notice, however, that the Au Bon Pain plan is not, in Kohn's words, "contingent on behavior." It is contingent on results, and herein lies the crucial difference. Plans that are contingent on behavior will encourage the prescribed behavior and stifle initiation. However, plans that reward desired results are likely to stimulate innovation.

> *"Incentives are neither all good nor all bad. Although not the right answer in all cases, they can be highly effective motivational tools."*
> —Donita S. Wolters

Perhaps the most disturbing omission from Kohn's article is his failure to suggest an alternative to the use of incentive plans. If companies are to abandon extrinsic incentives as a way to motivate employees, what are they to use instead? Is Kohn recommending that we live with the loss of individual motivation and lack of organizational innovation and flexibility that characterizes companies and societies without extrinsic incentives? Without some level of extrinsic incentive to supplement the intrinsic drive of individuals, organizations become unwieldy and inflexible. As a general prescription for the management of organizations, Kohn's approach is naive and utopian. In the real world, organizations must manage incentives if they are to be flexible, innovative, and directed.

DONITA S. WOLTERS
Manager of Human Resources, JMM Operational Services, Inc., Denver, Colorado

WHILE KOHN MAKES a number of valid points with respect to the dangers of incentive plans, his summary execution of incentives is unwarranted. Incentives are neither all good nor all bad. Although not the right answer in all cases, they can be highly effective motivational tools and should be employed under the appropriate circumstances.

Without a doubt, financial rewards can be, and have been, both overused and misused. Implementing a poorly designed or ill-suited incentive plan can do more harm than good because employees will inevitably receive mixed, even conflicting, messages from the organization about its values and priorities, leading to confusion and frustration. Incentives are no substitute for good management and should not be used indiscriminately to remedy problems when more effective solutions exist. Kohn mentions training and goal setting as examples of effective strategies for improving productivity, and his advice is well-taken. Incentives cannot improve performance if employees are not properly trained to perform their tasks or have no idea what is expected of them. But something more is often needed to elicit the necessary effort. The job-rate pay systems that typify unionized blue-collar environments—where mediocrity and lack of innovation are the hallmarks, and employees do just enough to get by—illustrate the point.

I have observed, as a veteran of many employee-counseling sessions, that employees are more apt to become disillusioned with incentive plans when they feel exploited because the expected rewards are not forthcoming, not when they are rewarded for something they were inclined to do in the first place. To avoid perceptions of exploitation and manipulation, however, two design features of the incentive program are imperative.

First, the criteria for and the actual evaluation of performance must be seen as objective and within the performer's control. This means that anyone should be able to predict the reward consistently and reliably based on given actions and results. The reward should not be determined through highly subjective processes, such as a supervisor's individual opinion. Kohn seems to support this view when he states that "not receiving a reward one had expected to receive is...indistinguishable from being punished."

Second, the recipient should consider the reward equal to the effort that produced it. Too insignificant and the incentive will be insulting and thus ineffective; overdone and the balance of fairness will be upset. Insufficient attention to these dynamics may underlie the apparent failure of many executive incentive plans, which could more accurately be termed entitlement programs.

Kohn goes on to decry the inability of incentives to "create an enduring *commitment* to any value or action." I question the relevance of this criticism. The purpose of incentives is not to change employees' values but to direct their behavior in ways that will benefit the organization and the employees themselves. More telling is

Kohn's failure to identify a viable alternative to incentives. Of course, the intrinsic rewards he praises are extremely motivating where they happen to exist, but they are not always present and cannot usually be created.

The current trend in organizations is toward less hierarchy and more teamwork. For employees, this means that fewer promotions are available and greater cooperation among coworkers is required. For employers, this means that maximum versatility and productivity must be summoned from all members. The use of incentive plans represents one strategy for aligning organizational and individual goals by treating employees as partners in both the risks and the successes of the business. Kohn recognizes that the majority of companies in the United States utilize some sort of incentive plan. Indeed, his assertions are being tested on the firing line and disproved by a persuasive cross section of U.S. business.

Alfie Kohn Responds

THE AVERAGE U.S. COMPANY has come to resemble a game show: "Tell our employees about the fabulous prizes we have for them if their productivity improves!" None of my respondents doubts the pervasiveness of this mentality. In fact, several profess incredulity that anyone would question the value of dangling rewards in front of people. In my experience, this reaction most often comes from the consultants who make their living selling incentive programs. What I hear around the country from people with no axe to grind is a frank acknowledgment that incentive plans rarely work.

Consider the following:

- A human-resource executive at a major U.S. auto company recently surveyed her colleagues in various industries; they told her that, at best, their incentive plans didn't do *too* much damage.

- *Training Magazine* ran a cover story in August: "Why No One Likes Your Incentive Program."

- As Michael Beer observes, pay-for-performance programs are typically tossed out a few years after they are begun.

- To the best of my knowledge, no controlled study has ever found long-term improvement in the quality of performance as a result of extrinsic rewards.

Of course, it is comforting to believe that incentives fail only for incidental reasons, such as that they are "misused," as Donita Wolters would have it, or that they are offered "for the wrong behavior," as George Baker claims. But I believe incentive plans *must* fail, because they are based on a patently inadequate theory of motivation. Trying to undo the damage by adopting a new pay-for-performance scheme is rather like trying to cure alcoholism by switching from vodka to gin. This argument makes a lot of people angry, as seems clear from Jerry McAdam's unpleasant speculations about my ulterior motives and from the amusing, if predictable, mutterings about communism by G. Bennett Stewart. If the attachment to carrot-and-stick psychology—or any dogma—is deep enough, questioning simply isn't permitted.

W. Edwards Deming, and others before him, have been telling us for years that money is not a motivator. Judging from Teresa Amabile's response, however, I may not have been clear enough about the difference between compensation in general and pay-for-performance in particular. Neither can produce quality, but only the latter is positively harmful. I agree with Amabile that "generous compensation . . . need not be seen as a bribe," but I disagree that "people do not always feel controlled by rewards." Richard Ryan and his colleagues at the University of Rochester, pioneers in researching this question, have concluded that "rewards in general appear to have a controlling significance to some extent and thus in general run the risk of undermining intrinsic motivation." Offering good things to people on the condition that they do what you tell them is, almost by definition, a way of trying to exert control.

But even someone who insists that it's possible in theory to devise a noncontrolling reward has to concede that control is what incentive plans in the real world are all about. Just listen to the defenders of these programs: the whole idea is to "direct [employees'] behavior," as Wolters says. No wonder the evidence shows that incentives do not "supplement the intrinsic drive of individuals," as Baker believes, but tend to supplant it. As a rule, the more salient the extrinsic motivator, the more intrinsic motivation evaporates.

One could say, as Baker does, that incentives work too well, in the sense that they are destructive of excellence and interest. But one cannot conclude from this that the problem is merely one of implementation. Baker errs in assuming that just because rewards undermine cooperation it follows that they can also create it. If something has the power to hurt, that doesn't mean more of it will motivate. Again, think of money: less of it can demotivate, but that doesn't mean that more of it will motivate. I think Baker also misunderstands why employees try so hard to convince their reward-dispensing supervisors that everything is under control. It's not because the latter are deliberately rewarding such behavior. Rather, the use of rewards and the extrinsic orientation they produce inexorably lead people to focus on pleasing those in charge of handing out the goodies. Fine-tuning the incentive plan cannot solve the problem.

Finally, a number of correspondents are understandably curious about my views on what should replace incentive plans. If a discussion on this point was conspicuously absent from the article, which was an excerpt from my book *Punished by Rewards,* it was due to limited space. I do grapple at length with alternatives to incentives in another chapter, "Thank God It's Monday." Here, a few words will have to suffice.

On compensation, my advice is this: pay people well and fairly, then do everything possible to help them forget about money. I have no objection to profit-sharing: it seems sensible enough that the people who made the profit ought to have it. Nor am I keen to promote one criterion for compensation over another: for example, need, seniority, job responsibilities, training, market value. My concern is primarily to convince managers to stop manipulating employees with rewards and punishments and to stop pushing money into their faces.

My other concern is to emphasize the futility of fiddling with compensation schemes. This is not the road to quality. Andrew Lebby, a consultant, and Eileen Appelbaum, a researcher, corroborate this, and each offers a way of thinking about where excellence actually comes from. I find it useful to think in terms of three C's: choice, collaboration, and content. Choice means that employees should be able to participate in making decisions about what they do every day. Collaboration denotes the need to structure teams in order to facilitate an exchange of ideas and a climate of support. Content refers to what people are asked to do: as Frederick Herzberg said, "If you want people motivated to do a good job, give them a good job to do."

An organization that provides these three ingredients in place of artificial inducements like incentive plans will not "lose its best people," as Beer worries. Innovation and excellence are the natural results of helping people experience intrinsic motivation. But intrinsic motivation cannot survive in an organization that treats its employees like pets.

Originally published in November–December 1993
Reprint 93610

A Simpler Way to Pay

EGON ZEHNDER

Executive Summary

THERE HAVE BEEN many changes in professional services since Egon Zehnder founded his executive search
firm nearly four decades ago—not the least of which has
been a shift in the way professionals pay themselves.
When he started, compensation everywhere was
strongly tied to seniority. Today, partners at most professional services firms are paid according to the size of
their client billings and their ability to bring in new clients.

But Egon Zehnder International, which now has 57
offices worldwide, has stuck with the old-fashioned way
to pay. In addition to giving partners base salaries and
equal shares in a percentage of the profit, the firm
apportions another fraction of the profit based only on
length of tenure as a partner. Yet the firm attracts outstanding consultants, and its turnover rate is low. The reasons, the author says, are simple: the firm's approach to

compensation forces it to hire team players—consultants who get more pleasure from the group's success than from their own advancements. And the seniority-based system requires the firm to find people who want to stay for the long haul. Call the system a relic, says Zehnder, but don't call it nonsense. It works.

In this article, the author describes the extremely intensive interview process used to hire the right kind of people. By the time the interviews are over, he says, potential hires know that people in the firm's Boston office think and act the same way as the people in its Brazil offices—and that they themselves must think and act that way if they are to succeed at the firm.

THERE HAVE BEEN many changes in professional services since the day I first set up shop in 1964—not the least of which has been a pronounced shift in the way professionals pay themselves. When I started, compensation was strongly tied to seniority. After all, seniority was a proxy for experience. Today, most consulting firms, law firms, and so forth consider seniority irrelevant—and occasionally something much worse. They believe pay should be based on performance and, more specifically, individual performance. That's why at most professional firms, people are paid according to the size of their client billings and how good they are at bringing in new clients. Indeed, firms invest considerable time and effort to measure those results precisely.

At Egon Zehnder International (EZI), we prefer to stick with the old-fashioned way to pay. In addition to base salaries, the firm gives partners equal shares of the profit and another set of profit shares that are adjusted only for length of tenure as partner. There is no formal procedure for tracking the performance of country offices, let alone individuals. At the close of a given year, for instance, a ten-year partner in any office will receive a larger share of the firm's profits than a five-year partner in any other office, even if the first office lost money and the second office broke billing records thanks entirely to the five-year partner's billings.

Our compensation system often prompts people to ask me how we manage to hire "stars," let alone keep them. They are shocked to learn that not only do we attract outstanding consultants year after year, but our annual turnover among partners is only 2%. (The industry average is 30%.) The reasons are simple, really. First, our approach to compensation forces us to hire consultants who have little interest in self-aggrandizement. We must hire people who are true team players, people who get more pleasure from the group's success than their own advancement. These individuals by nature tend to be highly collaborative. They eagerly share information and ideas about existing and potential clients. Similarly, they pass around information about the executives who might best meet a client's need. After all, if a consultant in Hamburg is paid according to overall firm performance, not her own billings, she will happily pick up the phone and call a colleague in New York to say, "I just met a candidate who isn't ideal for my client here. But he might be just perfect for your client's open position there."

Second, our seniority-based system requires us to find people who want to stay with a company for the long haul, for whatever reasons. Believe it or not, even in the new economy, these men and women still exist. And thank goodness for that. Nothing benefits a client and its executive search firm more than a consultant with a well-developed network of executive contacts and a finely honed intuition. By the time a consultant has worked more than a dozen years—as have 90 of our partners worldwide—he not only knows thousands of executives, he also knows the inner workings of hundreds of companies. In his brain and in his bones, he knows who should work where. He can make a match quickly and correctly. That makes clients very pleased indeed, which is perhaps why more than 60% of our assignments each year come from repeat clients.

That, then, is the business case for our simple approach to pay. We hire professionals who are not only highly educated—two academic degrees are a must—but who are also trustworthy and humble and who want to work for one company their entire careers. They naturally collaborate. The clients are delighted with the results, billings rise, and the profit pool expands—as it has for each of the 37 years since I founded the firm. In the end, everyone wins, from client to firm to individual professional. Call it a relic, but don't call it nonsense. It works.

Seniority Rules

EZI's seniority-based system is as easy to administer as it is to understand. For partners, compensation comes in three ways: salary, equity stake in EZI, and profit shares. There is some variation among partner salaries across countries because of variations in the cost of living; people don't expect to be paid the same base salary in Kuala Lumpur, say, that they would be paid in New York. But the distribution of equity and profits among the partners is consistent across the whole firm.

To begin with, each partner has an equal number of shares in the firm's equity, whether he has been a partner for 30 years or one year. The shares rise in value each year, because we put 10% to 20% of our profits back into the firm. When a partner retires or leaves the firm, he sells back the shares, keeping the difference between the value of his shares at the time of his election to partnership and their value at the time of his departure. Obviously, the longer you stay, the more valuable the shares become. If you stay for five years, your shares will probably double in value.

The remaining 80% to 90% of the profit is distributed among the partners in two ways. Sixty percent is divided equally among all the partners, and the remaining 40% is allocated according to years of seniority. Someone who has been partner for one year has one seniority year, a two-year partner has two seniority years, and so on up to 15 years, when a cap comes into effect. The pool is divided by the total number of seniority years to produce a base number; each partner receives an amount equal to that number multiplied by his seniority years. So a 15-year partner gets 15 times more from this portion of the profit pool than a one-year partner. (For a comparison of the compensations of a one-year and a 15-year partner, see the exhibit "Partners' Shares of the Profits.")

The seniority principle doesn't extend to consultants who are not yet partners, because they are still proving their partnership qualifications on many levels. Here we do apply a kind of performance-based approach: non-partner professionals get annual bonuses that are based on how well they have supported their colleagues and how they have contributed to the firm's reputation as a whole. But the performance we are measuring is not at all financial. For instance, if a consultant has published an article in a reputable business journal, it is marked to her credit because the contribution has benefited the Egon Zehnder reputation. At EZI, a consultant's annual bonus has nothing to do with the billings she has been

---

Partners' Shares of the Profits

EZI doesn't divulge the compensation of partners. But the mechanism for determining it is illustrated in this hypothetical example, which compares a one-year partner's equity increase and profit share with those of a 15-year partner.

Suppose EZI has a total of 100 partners with an accumulated seniority of 750 years, each partner has an equal number of shares in the firm, and EZI's profit after paying base salaries is $75 million. Ten percent of the profit is put back into the firm, increasing each partner's equity by one one-hundredth ($75,000) of that amount. The remaining $67.5 million is divided up: 60% is apportioned equally among the partners—each partner gets one one-hundredth, or $405,000—and 40% is allocated according to seniority. The 40% is divided by the total number of seniority years, 750, to produce a base number, $36,000; each partner receives an amount equal to the base number multiplied by his or her seniority years. The equity returns and profit shares of the two hypothetical partners are as follows.

Equity increase and profit share	1-year partner	15-year partner
Increase in equity value One one-hundredth of 10% of the $75 million profit	$75,000	$75,000
Share of equal-profit pool One one-hundredth of 60% of the profit remaining after 10% is put back into the firm	$405,000	$405,000
Share of seniority pool A figure based on years of seniority	$36,000	$540,000
Total	$516,000	$1,020,000

associated with and everything to do with how partner-like she has proved herself to be over the year.

The most immediate benefit of our system is that it is transparent and takes relatively little time to manage. By contrast, my closest friend is a senior partner at a large international law firm. He tells me that his firm has hardly any time for client work during the last month of the year because people are too busy deciding who gets how much bonus for which client. They have to work out who referred which project to whom and who developed and contributed to each project. How awful! They're not working for clients anymore—they're working for the compensation system.

A Fairer Way

The seniority rule for partner compensation has been in place ever since I founded EZI. From the start, I paid my first associate, Walter Siegenthaler, more than I paid my second associate, Hans Schaer, because I felt that Walter deserved more—to reflect the extra time and effort he had put into building the Egon Zehnder brand. That continued as the firm expanded and opened offices in Belgium, France, Britain, and so on.

As we grew, I became more convinced of the fairness of rewarding seniority. Financial performance is very heavily dependent on the immediate environment. Why should a hardworking partner in São Paulo be penalized because a downturn in the local economy has reduced the firm's billings in Brazil? At the same time, why should a partner in Hong Kong earn more because he was lucky enough to be parked in the center of the booming Asian economy?

The only exception to the seniority rule has been myself, for I have never been the highest earner in the firm. People might think that rather odd—after all, I am the founder. But I think it's fair. Initially at least, my associates had a far harder time than I did. It isn't easy for a consultant to work under a name that not only isn't his own but is hard to pronounce and has little recognition in the marketplace. Of course, that's changed now, and the firm has a global reputation. But back in the 1960s and 1970s, when I opened offices in London, Brussels, and Paris, hardly anyone could spell the name Egon Zehnder.

Making myself the exception has, in my opinion, helped to sustain acceptance of the system among my associates. It's easy for partners, especially the newer ones, to see seniority as a polite term for cronyism. That may be one reason seniority has gone out of favor at other firms. But, along with the 15-year cap on seniority benefits, my situation makes it impossible for anyone to argue that EZI's system is unfair.

Delivering Collaboration and Intuition

Of course, simplicity isn't everything. No matter how much time and effort we save by not measuring performance, no compensation system can work unless it promotes the right kind of behavior among professionals. Proponents of pay-for-individual-performance systems argue that their plans encourage managers to generate more revenue, which more than compensates for any administrative burdens the systems may impose. But those systems have one great drawback: they encourage people to further their own interests ahead of the interests of clients and the organization as a whole.

Picture this typical scenario. A New York conglomerate needs to find a manager for its Spanish subsidiary. At most executive search firms—the ones that reward individual performance—the consultant who gets the assignment will hang onto it tooth and nail. It doesn't matter if the consultant is based in New York. He will fly to Madrid every week, if he has to, in order to locate the right candidate for the position. Yes, he may stop into the firm's Spanish office. He may even chat with its consultants about leads. But he will take the time—billing hourly, in many cases—to complete the job himself.

At EZI, no consultant would dream of such hoarding. Contacted by the conglomerate, he would immediately pass the assignment to the local office in Spain, where it could be completed with the kind of speed and accuracy clients seem to adore. He would also invest time and energy in making sure that the Spanish office understood the new client's interests and needs. At the end of the year, all would share equally in the larger profit that resulted.

Or consider this story, which happened just recently. The CEO of a German client that needed a manager for a textile company in Bavaria came to a partner in our Zurich office whom he had worked with before. Because of the past relationship, the Swiss partner would have liked very much to help the client, and if he had been concerned about his individual billings, all the more so. But instead, the partner referred the client to a person in our Munich office who was much better qualified

Seniority is unfashionable, especially in America, which worships youth and energy. But our system helps us build the right kind of human capital for our profession.

to help. The Munich partner knew the industry inside out, and he had a feel for Bavaria's idiosyncrasies. The match was so successful that the client ended up hiring not only the manager he wanted but also one of the other candidates the Munich partner had put forward. The client is all the more likely to come to EZI again, because he knows we will give our very best.

Any firm in our profession that is serious about putting the client's need first has to be able to support the client with its whole network. Executive talent is a global resource: a company in New York might hire a Frenchman whose previous jobs were in Brazil and Japan. The firm should assign the most qualified people in the most qualified offices, regardless of whose contact the client initially was.

Our system, by rewarding seniority, also helps us build the right kind of human capital for our profession. I know that seniority is a very unfashionable idea these days, especially in America, which worships youth and energy. But in our profession, seniority is a key asset: it is only through experience that our consultants can hone the intuition they need to operate successfully in a people-intensive profession.

It is also through length of service that a consultant builds a strong network of contacts. Senior search consultants not only know a great many people, they also know them very well, which means that their hunches are taken seriously. Let's say, for example, that I really believed that the émigré taxi driver who took me from the airport yesterday was the right person to head P&G's operations in Russia. I would have no problem telling that to the head of P&G Europe because I have known him for years and have found many of his key executives.

He would take me seriously. But 30 years ago, he would have responded with no more than a sarcastic smile.

Finding the Right People

For our system to work successfully, we have to hire the right kind of people. But how? First, our interview process is extremely intensive. We see many hundreds of people each year, mainly graduates of the leading business schools, of whom only a small fraction are hired. Each candidate sees between 25 and 30 consultants during the process—old partners, young partners, and new associates. Our people have a good look at the applicant, and if any of them expresses serious reservations, we usually do not make an offer. What's more, by the time the interviews are over, potential hires realize that they are hearing more than a sales pitch about the firm. They know that the people in our Boston office think and act the same way as the people in our British and Brazilian offices, and that they themselves must think and act that way if they are to be successful at EZI.

Until recently, when I retired, I interviewed every candidate myself. I used to ask people bluntly: "Do you know that even if you have the highest billings in the firm and are responsible for 60% of the profits of your office, you won't get an extra penny for it? Picture yourself in that situation. Are you comfortable with it? If you aren't, don't join us. You'll be very unhappy." After more than 40 years in the profession, I can usually tell if their answers are sincere. A really good actor can always fool me, of course, but I get it right 90% of the time. (For more on my interview approach, see "No Ordinary Interview" at the end of this article.)

We also take much more time to promote people to partner than do most consulting firms. At EZI, people work for five or more years before they are considered for partnership. During that period, we observe people very closely—not to see how many clients they are bringing in, but to make sure they are hardworking, honest, collaborative, and entrepreneurial. We want to know whether the partners in a candidate's office believe that he or she should have the same stake in the firm as they have. Has the prospect ever passed clients on to Copenhagen? Is he an active alumnus of his university? Does he publish articles or give speeches? The decision on whom to put up for partnership is made by a group of partners drawn from all of our offices every three years. This Partnership Evaluation Group has the authority to call on anyone who has had contact with a candidate for partnership: colleagues in the candidate's office, colleagues in other offices, even clients.

Making partner at Egon Zehnder is not an easy process, and it's expensive for the firm. But we have become very good at it: of the ten to 20 people put up for partner each year, only one or two will fail to make the grade. What's more, those partners will often stay for their entire professional careers, to the benefit of both our clients and the firm, amply returning our investment in their selection.

At the end of the day, I wouldn't recommend that every company copy our system too closely. It is probably not appropriate in most industrial corporations, where there can be big differences in the types of work that people do. You would not expect to reward the head of R&D, for instance, the same way you reward the head of sales.

But at professional services firms, the work is quite homogeneous—what a lawyer does in Tokyo, for instance, isn't all that different from what a lawyer does in Zurich. In these cases, I think that a compensation system such as ours, which reinforces common values and sets common expectations, has much to recommend it. EZI's record of nearly 40 years of ever-increasing profits certainly suggests as much.

A Different Way of Charging

MOST EXECUTIVE SEARCH FIRMS charge a client a percentage of the first year's salary of any person who is recruited through the firm. This creates pressure to find people who can command high salaries because of their track records but who may not be right for the positions involved.

At EZI, we avoid this conflict of interest by charging a flat fee agreed to in advance for our searches. The fee is calculated according to both the importance of the position and our best estimate of the difficulty of the work involved. We look, for instance, at whether the industry is new to the country of search, at the number of companies we can go to in order to find candidates for our client, and at the language skills candidates will need. We don't always guess right, of course, and often we find ourselves undercharging because the job has proved more complex than it first seemed.

But our clients appreciate the efforts we make on their behalf, and they recognize that our flat fee encourages EZI to find the right candidates—people who will stay and be productive over the long term—rather than the most expensive ones. So they will probably come back to us in the future with assignments that will prove simpler than they first appear; when all is said and done, that will leave us even.

No Ordinary Interview

Although there are probably few "experts" who would recommend it, I ask very personal questions when I interview people. If an applicant is married, for instance, I might ask her how she met her husband and why she decided to marry him. I ask these questions partly because they are the only ones left to ask—my colleagues have already asked all the technical and professional questions. But I also ask them because the answers to personal questions can often tell me what a person's values are and how he or she makes important choices.

There are no right or wrong answers to my questions, and people can give totally different answers to the ones I would give. And I'm not looking for demonstrations of intellectual brilliance—my colleagues have already done that. What I am looking for is integrity. I want answers that make me feel that the person is warm, honest, and sincere. Those qualities are very important in a collaborative partnership like EZI.

So when I ask an applicant why he went to a particular school, for instance, I'd rather hear him say that he went to Michigan State because he thought he couldn't get into Harvard or Stanford than that he picked Michigan State because it was good in a particular field. When I ask why he thinks he would be happy at EZI, I don't want to hear him say that he thinks he can create more value in EZI than he can anywhere else. What does "create more value" really mean? It is so often an insincere cliché. Do people really change jobs because they can't add enough value?

Some people—particularly Americans—find my questions intrusive and too personal (that's one reason I always interview in Zurich). But I want to look inside a person as deeply as I can because that person may well be in the firm for the rest of his or her professional life.

Originally published in April 2001
Reprint R0104B

What You Need to Know About Stock Options

BRIAN J. HALL

Executive Summary

STOCK OPTION GRANTS have come to dominate the pay of top executives. But while they've made many people wealthy, their impact on business in general remains controversial. Critics say options motivate corporate leaders to boost stock values in the short run rather then build companies that will thrive over the long run.

Drawing on an extensive analysis of the real-world impact of options, Brian Hall argues that the critics are wrong. Option grants are the best compensation mechanism we have for getting managers to act in ways that ensure the long-term success of their companies and the well-being of workers and stockholders.

But because options tend to be poorly understood, companies often end up with counterproductive plans. The author explains the three types of option plans that can be used. Fixed value plans, for which executives receive options of a predetermined value every year, are ideal for companies that set pay according to compensation surveys, but they weaken the link between pay and performance. Fixed number plans, which stipulate the number of options executives will receive over the plan period, provide a much stronger link. The lumpsum megagrant is the most highly leveraged type of grant because it not only fixes the number of options in advance, it fixes the exercise price as well. The type of plan must be carefully matched to the company's strategy.

The article is accompanied by several exhibits, including a chart entitled "Which Plans?" that succinctly sets out the weaknesses and strengths of each type of option program.

T WENTY YEARS AGO, the biggest component of executive compensation was cash, in the form of salaries and bonuses. Stock options were just a footnote. Now the reverse is true. With astounding speed, stock option grants have come to dominate the pay—and often the wealth—of top executives throughout the United States. Last year, Jack Welch's unexercised GE options were valued at more than $260 million. Intel CEO Craig Barrett's were worth more than $100 million. Michael Eisner exercised 22 million options on Disney stock in 1998 alone, netting more than a half-billion dollars. In total, U.S. executives hold unexercised options worth tens of billions of dollars.

It would be difficult to exaggerate how much the options explosion has changed corporate America. But has the change been for the better or for the worse? Certainly, option grants have improved the fortunes of many individual executives, entrepreneurs, software engineers, and investors. Their long-term impact on business in general remains much less clear, however. Even some of the people who have profited most from the trend express a deep discomfort about their companies' growing dependence on options. Do we really know what we're doing? they ask. Are the incentives we're creating in line with our business goals? What's going to happen when the bull market ends?

Option grants are even more controversial for many outside observers. The grants seem to shower ever greater riches on top executives, with little connection to corporate performance. They appear to offer great upside rewards with little downside risk. And, according to some very vocal critics, they motivate corporate leaders to pursue short-term moves that provide immediate boosts to stock values rather than build companies that will thrive over the long run. As the use of stock options has begun to expand internationally, such concerns have spread from the United States to the business centers of Europe and Asia.

I have been studying the use of option grants for a number of years now, modeling how their values change under different circumstances, evaluating how they interact with other forms of compensation, and examining how the various programs support or undermine companies' business goals. What I've found is that the critics of options are mistaken. Options do not promote a selfish, near-term perspective on the part of businesspeople. Quite the contrary. Options are the best compensation mechanism we have for getting managers to act in ways that ensure the long-term success of their companies and the well-being of their workers and stockholders.

But I've also found that the general nervousness about options is well warranted. Stock options are bafflingly complex financial instruments. (See "A Short Course on Options and Their Valuation" at the end of this article.) They tend to be poorly understood by both those who grant them and those who receive them. As a result, companies often end up having option programs that are counterproductive. I have, for example, seen many Silicon Valley companies continue to use their pre-IPO programs—with unfortunate consequences—after the companies have grown and gone public. And I've seen many large, sleepy companies use option programs that unwittingly create weak incentives for innovation and value creation. The lesson is clear: it's not enough just to have an option program; you need to have the right program.

Before discussing the strengths and weaknesses of different types of programs, I'd like to step back and examine why option grants are, in general, an extraordinarily powerful form of compensation.

The Pay-to-Performance Link

The main goal in granting stock options is, of course, to tie pay to performance—to ensure that executives profit when their companies prosper and suffer when they flounder. Many critics claim that, in practice, option grants have not fulfilled that goal. Executives, they argue, continue to be rewarded as handsomely for failure as for success. As evidence, they either use anecdotes—examples of poorly performing companies that compensate their top managers extravagantly—or they cite studies indicating that the total pay of executives in charge of high-performing companies is not much different from the pay of those heading poor performers. The anecdotes are hard to dispute—some companies do act foolishly in paying their executives—but they don't prove much. The studies are another matter. Virtually all of them share a fatal flaw: they measure only the compensation earned in a given year. What's left out is the most important component of the pay-to-performance link—the appreciation or depreciation of an executive's holdings of stock and options.

As executives at a company receive yearly option grants, they begin to amass large amounts of stock and unexercised options. The value of those holdings appreciates greatly when the company's stock price rises and depreciates just as greatly when it falls. When the shifts in value of the overall holdings are taken into account, the link between pay and performance becomes much clearer. Indeed, in a study I conducted with Jeffrey Liebman of Harvard's Kennedy School of Government, we found that changes in stock and stock option valuations account for 98% of the link between pay and performance for the average chief executive, while annual salary and bonus payments account for a mere 2%.

By increasing the number of shares executives control, option grants have dramatically strengthened the link between pay and performance. Take a look at the exhibit "Tying Pay to Performance." It shows how two measures of the pay-to-performance link have changed since 1980. One measure is the amount by which an average CEO's wealth changes when his company's market value changes by $1,000. The other measure shows the amount by which CEO wealth changes with a 10% change in company value. For both measures, the link between pay and performance has increased nearly

Tying Pay to Performance

The estimated link between pay and performance has increased dramatically since 1980.

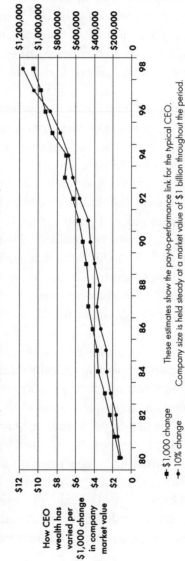

These estimates show the pay-to-performance link for the typical CEO. Company size is held steady at a market value of $1 billion throughout the period.

■ $1,000 change
● 10% change

tenfold since 1980. While there are many reasons American companies have flourished over the last two decades, it's no coincidence that the boom has come in the wake of the shift in executive pay from cash to equity. In stark contrast to the situation 20 years ago, when most executives tended to be paid like bureaucrats and act like bureaucrats, today's executives are much more likely to be paid like owners and act like owners.

Given the complexity of options, though, it is reasonable to ask a simple question: if the goal is to align the incentives of owners and managers, why not just hand out shares of stock? The answer is that options provide far greater leverage. For a company with an average dividend yield and a stock price that exhibits average volatility, a single stock option is worth only about one-third of the value of a share. That's because the option holder receives only the incremental appreciation above the exercise price, while the stockholder receives all the value, plus dividends. The company can therefore give an executive three times as many options as shares for the same cost. The larger grant dramatically increases the impact of stock price variations on the executive's wealth. (In addition to providing leverage, options offer accounting advantages. See "Accounting for Options" at the end of this article.)

The idea of using leveraged incentives is not new. Most salespeople, for example, are paid a higher commission rate on the revenues they generate above a certain target. For instance, they might receive 2% of sales up to $1 million and 10% of sales above $1 million. Such plans are more difficult to administer than plans with a single commission rate, but when it comes to compensation, the advantages of leverage often outweigh the disadvantages of complexity.

The Downside Risk

If pay is truly to be linked to performance, it's not enough to deliver rewards when results are good. You also have to impose penalties for weak performance. The critics claim options have unlimited upside but no downside. The implicit assumption is that options have no value when granted and that the recipient thus has nothing to lose. But that assumption is completely false. Options do have value. Just look at the financial exchanges, where options on stock are bought and sold for large sums of money every second. Yes, the value of option grants is illiquid and, yes, the eventual payoff is contingent on the future performance of the company. But they have value nonetheless. And if something has value that can be lost, it has, by definition, downside risk.

In fact, options have even greater downside risk than stock. Consider two executives in the same company. One is granted a million dollars worth of stock, and the other is granted a million dollars worth of at-the-money options—options whose exercise price matches the stock price at the time of the grant. If the stock price falls sharply, say by 75%, the executive with stock has lost $750,000, but she retains $250,000. The executive with options, however, has essentially been wiped out. His options are now so far under water that they are nearly worthless. Far from eliminating penalties, options actually amplify them.

The downside risk has become increasingly evident to executives as their pay packages have come to be dominated by options. Take a look at the employment contract Joseph Galli negotiated with Amazon.com when he recently agreed to become the e-tailer's COO. In addition to a large option grant, his contract contains a protection clause that requires Amazon to pay him up to $20 million if his options don't pay off. One could argue that providing such protection to executives is foolish from a shareholder's point of view, but the contract itself makes an important point: why would someone need such protection if options had no downside risk?

The risk inherent in options can be undermined, however, through the practice of repricing. When a stock price falls sharply, the issuing company can be tempted to reduce the exercise price of previously granted options in order to increase their value for the executives who hold them. Such repricing is anathema to shareholders, who don't enjoy the privilege of having their shares repriced. Although fairly common in small companies—especially those in Silicon Valley—option repricing is relatively rare for senior managers of large companies, despite some well-publicized exceptions. In 1998, fewer than 2% of all large companies repriced any options for their top executive teams. Even for companies that had large decreases in their stock prices—declines of 25% or worse in the previous year—the repricing rate was less than 5%. And only 8% of companies with market-value declines of more than 50% repriced. In most cases, companies that resorted to repricing could have avoided the need to do so by using a different kind of option program, as I'll discuss later.

Promoting the Long View

It's often assumed that when you tie compensation to stock price, you encourage executives to take a short-term focus. They end up spending so much time trying to make sure that the next quarter's results meet or beat Wall Street's expectations that they lose sight of what's in the best long-term interests of their companies. Again, however, the criticism does not stand up to close examination.

For a method of compensation to motivate managers to focus on the long term, it needs to be tied to a performance measure that looks forward rather than backward. The traditional measure—accounting profits—fails that test. It measures the past, not the future. Stock price, however, is a forward-looking measure. It forecasts how current actions will affect a company's future profits. Forecasts can never be completely accurate, of course. But because investors have their own money on the line, they face enormous pressure to read the future correctly. That makes the stock market the best predictor of performance we have.

But what about the executive who has a great long-term strategy that is not yet fully appreciated by the market? Or, even worse, what about the executive who can fool the market by pumping up earnings in the short run while hiding fundamental problems? Investors may be the best forecasters we have, but they are not omniscient. Option grants provide an effective means for addressing these risks: slow vesting. In most cases, executives can only exercise their options in stages over an extended period—for example, 25% per year over four years. That delay serves to reward managers who take actions with longer-term payoffs while exacting a harsh penalty on those who fail to address basic business problems.

Stock options are, in short, the ultimate forward-looking incentive plan—they measure future cash flows, and, through the use of vesting, they measure them in the future as well as in the present. They don't create managerial myopia; they help to cure it. If a company wants to encourage a more farsighted perspective, it should not abandon option grants—it should simply extend their vesting periods.[1]

Three Types of Plans

Most of the companies I've studied don't pay a whole lot of attention to the way they grant options. Their directors and executives assume that the important thing is just to have a plan in place; the details are trivial. As a result, they let their HR departments or compensation consultants decide on the form of the plan, and they rarely examine the available alternatives. Often, they aren't even aware that alternatives exist.

But such a laissez-faire approach, as I've seen over and over again, can lead to disaster. The way options are granted has an enormous impact on a company's efforts to achieve its business goals. While option plans can take many forms, I find it useful to divide them into three types. The first two—what I call fixed value plans and fixed number plans—extend over several years. The third—megagrants—consists of onetime lump sum distributions. The three types of plans provide very different incentives and entail very different risks.

FIXED VALUE PLANS

With fixed value plans, executives receive options of a predetermined value every year over the life of the plan. A company's board may, for example, stipulate that the CEO will receive a $1 million grant annually for the next three years. Or it may tie the value to some percentage of the executive's cash compensation, enabling the grant to grow as the executive's salary or salary plus bonus increases. The value of the options is typically determined using Black-Scholes or similar valuation formulas, which take into account such factors as the number of years until the option expires, prevailing interest rates, the volatility of the stock price, and the stock's dividend rate.

Fixed value plans are popular today. That's not because they're intrinsically better than other plans— they're not—but because they enable companies to carefully control the compensation of executives and the percentage of that compensation derived from option grants. Fixed value plans are therefore ideal for the many companies that set executive pay according to studies performed by compensation consultants that document how much comparable executives are paid and in what form.[2] By adjusting an executive's pay package every year to keep it in line with other executives' pay, companies hope to minimize what the consultants call "retention risk"—the possibility that executives will jump ship for new posts that offer more attractive rewards.

But fixed value plans have a big drawback. Because they set the value of future grants in advance, they weaken the link between pay and performance. Executives end up receiving fewer options in years of strong performance (and high stock values) and more options in years of weak performance (and low stock values). To see how that works, let's look at the pay of a hypothetical CEO whom I'll call John. As part of his pay plan, John receives $1 million in at-the-money options each year. In the first year, the company's stock price is $100, and John receives about 28,000 options. Over the next year, John succeeds in boosting the company's stock price to $150. As a result, his next $1 million grant includes only 18,752 options. The next year, the stock price goes up another $50. John's grant falls again, to 14,000 options. The stock price has doubled; the number of options John receives has been cut in half. (The exhibit "The Impact of Different Option Plans on Compensation" summarizes the effect of stock price changes on the three kinds of plans.)

Now let's look at what happens to John's grants when his company performs miserably. In the first year, the stock price falls from $100 to $65. John's $1 million grant provides him with 43,000 options, up considerably from the original 28,000. The stock price continues to plummet the next year, falling to just $30. John's grant jumps to nearly 94,000 options. He ends up, in other words, being given a much larger piece of the company that he appears to be leading toward ruin.

It's true that the value of John's existing holdings of options and shares will vary considerably with changes in stock price. But the annual grants themselves are insulated from the company's performance—in much the same way that salaries are. For that reason, fixed value plans provide the weakest incentives of the three types of programs. I call them low-octane plans.

FIXED NUMBER PLANS

Whereas fixed value plans stipulate an annual value for the options granted, fixed number plans stipulate the number of options the executive will receive over the plan period. Under a fixed number plan, John would receive 28,000 at-the-money options in each of the three years, regardless of what happened to the stock price. Here, obviously, there is a much stronger link between pay and performance. Since the value of at-the-money options changes with the stock price, an increase in the stock price today increases the value of future option

The Impact of Different Option Plans on Compensation

Option values are derived using the Black-Scholes model and reflect the characteristics of a typical but hypothetical Fortune 500 company; the annual standard deviation of the stock price is assumed to be 32%, the risk-free rate of return is 6%, the dividend rate is 3%, and the maturity period is ten years.

			Stock price increase			Stock price decrease	
		Year 1 $100	Year 2 $150	Year 3 $200	Year 3 $200	Year 2 $65	Year 3 $30
	Stock price						
Fixed value plan	Options granted	28,128	18,752	14,064		43,273	93,759
	Value of options	$1 million	$1 million	$1 million		$1 million	$1 million
	Cumulative value			$5.4 million			$1.3 million
Fixed number plan	Options granted	28,128	28,128	28,128		28,128	28,128
	Value of options	$1 million	$1.5 million	$2 million		$650,000	$300,000
	Cumulative value			$7.2 million			$510,000
Megagrant plan	Options granted	79,697	0	0		0	0
	Value of options	$2.8 million	0	0		0	0
	Cumulative value			$8.1 million			$211,000

grants. Likewise, a decrease in stock price reduces the value of future option grants. For John, boosting the stock price 100% over two years would increase the value of his annual grant from $1 million in the first year to $2 million in the third. A 70% drop in the stock price, by contrast, would reduce the value of his grant to just $300,000.

Since fixed number plans do not insulate future pay from stock price changes, they create more powerful incentives than fixed value plans. I call them medium-octane plans, and, in most circumstances, I recommend them over their fixed value counterparts.

MEGAGRANT PLANS

Now for the high-octane model: the lump-sum mega-grant. While not as common as the multiyear plans, megagrants are widely used among private companies and post-IPO high-tech companies, particularly in Silicon Valley. Megagrants are the most highly leveraged type of grant because they not only fix the number of options in advance, they also fix the exercise price. To continue with our example, John would receive, at the start of the first year, a single megagrant of nearly 80,000 options, which has a Black-Scholes value of $2.8 million (equivalent to the net present value of $1 million per year for three years). Shifts in stock price have a dramatic effect on this large holding. If the stock price doubles, the value of John's options jumps to $8.1 million. If the price drops 70%, his options are worth a mere $211,000, less than 8% of the original stake.

Disney's Michael Eisner is perhaps the best known CEO who has received megagrants. Every few years since 1984, Eisner has received a megagrant of several million shares. It is the leverage of these packages, coupled with the large gains in Disney's stock during the last 15 years, that has made Eisner so fabulously wealthy.

The Big Trade-Off

Since the idea behind options is to gain leverage and since megagrants offer the most leverage, you might conclude that all companies should abandon multiyear plans and just give high-octane megagrants. Unfortunately, it's not so simple. The choice among plans involves a complicated trade-off between providing strong incentives today and ensuring that strong incentives will still exist tomorrow, particularly if the company's stock price falls substantially.

When viewed in those terms, megagrants have a big problem. Look at what happened to John in our third scenario. After two years, his megagrant was so far under water that he had little hope of making much money on it, and it thus provided little incentive for boosting the stock value. And he was not receiving any new at-the-money options to make up for the worthless ones—as he would have if he were in a multiyear plan. If the drop in stock value was a result of poor management, John's pain would be richly deserved. If, however, the drop was related to overall market volatility—or if the stock had been overvalued when John took charge—then John's suffering would be dangerous for the company. It would provide him with a strong motivation to quit, join a new company, and get some new at-the-money options.

Ironically, the companies that most often use megagrants—high-tech start-ups—are precisely those most likely to endure such a worst-case scenario. Their stock

prices are highly volatile, so extreme shifts in the value of
their options are commonplace. And since their people
are in high demand, they are very likely to head for
greener pastures when their megagrants go bust. Indeed,
Silicon Valley is full of megagrant companies that have
experienced human resources crises in response to stock
price declines. Such companies must choose between
two bad alternatives: they can reprice their options,
which undermines the integrity of all future option plans
and upsets shareholders, or they can refrain from repricing and watch their demoralized employees head out
the door.

Adobe Systems, Apple Computer, E'Trade, Netscape,
PeopleSoft, and Sybase have all repriced their options in
recent years, despite the bad will it creates among shareholders. As one Silicon Valley executive told me, "You
have to reprice. If you don't, employees will walk across
the street and reprice themselves."

Silicon Valley companies could avoid many such situations by using multiyear plans. So why don't they? The
answer lies in their heritage. Before going public, start-
ups find the use of megagrants highly attractive.
Accounting and tax rules allow them to issue options at
significantly discounted exercise prices. These "penny
options" have little chance of falling under water (especially in the absence of the stock price volatility created
by public markets). The risk profile of these pre-IPO
grants is actually closer to that of shares of stock than to
the risk profile of what we commonly think of as options.

When they go public, the companies continue to use
megagrants out of habit and without much consideration of the alternatives. But now they issue at-the-money
options. As we've seen, the risk profile of at-the-money

options on highly volatile stocks is extremely high. What had been an effective way to reward key people suddenly has the potential to demotivate them or even spur them to quit.

Some high-tech executives claim that they have no choice—they need to offer megagrants to attract good people. Yet in most cases, a fixed number grant (of comparable value) would provide an equal enticement with far less risk. With a fixed number grant, after all, you still guarantee the recipient a large number of options; you simply set the exercise prices for portions of the grant at different intervals. By staggering the exercise prices in this way, the value of the package becomes more resilient to drops in the stock price.

Many of the Silicon Valley executives (and potential executives) that I have talked to worry a lot about joining post-IPO companies at the wrong time, when the companies' stock prices are temporarily overvalued. Switching to multiyear plans or staggering the exercise prices of megagrants are good ways to reduce the potential for a value implosion.

Sleepy Companies, Sleepy Plans

Small, highly volatile Silicon Valley companies are not the only ones that are led astray by old habits. Large, stable, well-established companies also routinely choose the wrong type of plan. But they tend to default to multiyear plans, particularly fixed value plans, even though they would often be better served by megagrants.

Think about your average big, bureaucratic company. The greatest threat to its well-being is not the loss of a few top executives (indeed, that might be the best thing that could happen to it). The greatest threat is compla-

cency. To thrive, it needs to constantly shake up its organization and get its managers to think creatively about
new opportunities to generate value. The high-octane
incentives of megagrants are ideally suited to such situations, yet those companies hardly ever consider them.
Why not? Because the companies are dependent on consultants' compensation surveys, which invariably lead
them to adopt the low-octane but highly predictable
fixed value plans. (See the exhibit "Which Plan?")

The bad choices made by both incumbents and
upstarts reveal how dangerous it is for executives and
board members to ignore the details of the type of option
plan they use. While options in general have done a great
deal to get executives to think and act like owners, not
all option plans are created equal. Only by building a
clear understanding of how options work—how they
provide different incentives under different circumstances, how their form affects their function, how various factors influence their value—will a company be able
to ensure that its option program is actually accomplish-
ing its goals. If distributed in the wrong way, options are
no better than traditional forms of executive pay. In
some situations, they may be considerably worse.

A Short Course on Options and Their Valuation

EXECUTIVE STOCK OPTIONS are "call" options. They
give the holder the right, but not the obligation, to purchase a company's shares at a specified price—the
"exercise" or "strike" price. In the vast majority of cases,
options are granted "at the money," which means that

Which Plan?

Plan	Definition	Example	Strenghts	Weaknesses	Comments on applicability
Fixed value	A series of annual grants whose value is held constant or maintained at a fixed proportion of salary or total cash compensation.	An executive is granted $1 million worth of options each year for four years or is given a grant with a value equal to 1.2 times salary each year for four years.	Minimizes retention risk: even if the stock price falls significantly, the executive is given a large new grant the following year, ensuring that he or she always holds a significant equity stake.	Low-octane: creates the weakest incentives for value creation.	Poorly suited to large, stagnant companies that lack entrepreneurial drive. Often appropriate for nonexecutive employees, where the minimization of retention risk is often at least as important as the value-creation incentives.

Plan	Definition	Example	Strengths	Weaknesses	Comments on applicability
Fixed number	A series of annual grants of a fixed number of options.	An executive is granted 25,000 at-the-money options each year for four years.	Creates higher-powered incentives than fixed value plans; new at-the-money options each year reduce retention risk.	Provides lower-octane incentives than megagrants; has higher retention risk than fixed value plans since it provides a smaller option grant to an executive following a stock-price decline.	Can provide a nice balance between high-powered incentives and low retention risk for many companies. Well suited to post-IPO start-ups that are currently using megagrants. Along with megagrants, may be ideal for companies that are currently using fixed value plans and want to create stronger incentives for value creation.
Megagrant	A large, up-front grant in lieu of annual grants; the exercise price and the number of options are fixed at the time of the grant.	An executive is granted 100,000 at-the-money options this year and none in the next three years.	High-octane: creates the most high-powered incentives for value creation.	Exacerbates retention risk: if the stock price falls significantly, executives have weak incentives and may depart unless their options are repriced.	Well suited to large, stable companies that need infusions of entrepreneurial vigor, particularly those that are unlikely to face high retention risk in the event of a drop in stock price. Not well suited to post-IPO high-tech start-ups with volatile stock prices and a need to retain key executives.

the exercise price matches the stock price at the time of the grant. A small minority of options are granted "out of the money," with an exercise price higher than the stock price—these are premium options. An even smaller minority are granted "in the money," with an exercise price lower than the stock price—these are discount options.

The options issued to executives usually have important restrictions. They can't be sold to a third party, and they must be exercised before a defined maturity date, which is typically ten years from the grant date. Most, but not all, have a vesting period, usually of between three and five years; the option holder does not actually own the option, and therefore may not exercise it, until the option vests. Option holders do not usually receive dividends, which means they make a profit only on any appreciation of the stock price beyond the exercise price.

The value of an option is typically measured with the Black-Scholes pricing model or some variation. Black-Scholes provides a good estimate of the price an executive could receive for an option if he could sell it. Since such an option cannot be sold, its actual value to an executive is typically less than its Black-Scholes value.[3] Nevertheless, understanding Black-Scholes valuations is helpful because they provide a useful benchmark.

Black-Scholes takes account of the many factors that affect the value of an option—not only the stock price, but also the exercise price, the maturity date, the prevailing interest rates, the volatility of the company's stock, and the company's dividend rate. The last two factors—volatility and dividend rate—are particularly important because they vary greatly from company to company and have a large influence on option value. Let's look at each of them:

Volatility

The higher the volatility of a company's stock price, the higher the value of its options. The logic here is that while the owner of an option will receive the full value of any upside change, the downside is limited—an option's pay-off hits zero once the stock price falls to the exercise price, but if the stock falls further, the option's payoff remains at zero. (That's not to say that options have no down-side. They lose their value quickly and can end up worth nothing.) The higher expected payoff raises the option's value. But the potential for higher payoff is not without a cost—higher volatility makes the payoff riskier to the executive.

Dividend Rate

The higher a company's dividend rate, the lower the value of its options. Companies reward their shareholders in two ways: by increasing the price of their stock and by paying dividends. Most option holders, however, do not receive dividends; they are rewarded only through price appreciation. Since a company that pays high dividends has less cash for buying back shares or profitably reinvesting in its business, it will have less share-price appreciation, all other things being equal. There-fore, it provides a lower return to option holders. Research by Christine Jolls of Harvard Law School sug-gests, in fact, that the options explosion is partially responsible for the decline in dividend rates and the increase in stock repurchases during the past decade.

The chart "The Effect of Volatility and Dividend Rate on Option Value" shows how changes in volatility and dividend rate affect the value of an at-the-money option with a ten-year maturity. For a company with 30% volatil-ity—about the average for the *Fortune 500*—and a 2%

dividend rate, an option is worth about 40% of the price of a share of stock. Increase the volatility to 70%, and the option's value goes up to 64% of the stock price. Decrease the dividend rate to 0, and the option's value goes up to 56%. Do both, and the option's value shoots up to 81%.

It's important to note that Black-Scholes is just a formula; it's not a method for picking stocks. It can't, and makes no attempt to, make predictions about which companies will perform well and which will perform poorly. In the end, the factor that will determine an option's payoff is the change in the price of the underlying stock. If you are an executive, you can raise the value of your options by taking actions that increase the value of the stock. That's the whole idea of option grants.

Accounting for Options

UNDER CURRENT ACCOUNTING rules, as long as the number and exercise price of options are fixed in advance, their cost never hits the P&L. That is, options are not treated as an expense, either when they're granted or when they're exercised. The accounting treatment of options has generated enormous controversy. On one side are some shareholders who argue that because options are compensation and compensation is an expense, options should show up on the P&L. On the other side are many executives, especially those in small companies, who counter that options are difficult to value properly and that expensing them would discourage their use.

The response of institutional investors to the special treatment of options has been relatively muted. They have not been as critical as one might expect. There are two reasons for this. First, companies are required to list their option expenses in a footnote to the balance sheet, so savvy investors can easily figure option costs into expenses. Even more important, activist shareholders have been among the most vocal in pushing companies to replace cash pay with options. They don't want to do anything that might turn companies back in the other direction.

In my view, the worst thing about the current accounting rules is not that they allow companies to avoid listing options as an expense. It's that they treat different types of option plans differently, for no good reason. That discourages companies from experimenting with new kinds of plans. As just one example, the accounting rules penalize discounted, indexed options—options with an exercise price that is initially set beneath the current stock

---

The Effect of Volatility and Dividend Rate on Option Value

Option value is stated as a fraction of stock price. Volatility is stated as the annual standard deviation of the company's stock-price returns. The figures assume a ten-year at-the-money option with a prevailing risk-free rate (ten-year bond rate) of 6%. For Fortune 500 companies, 30% volatility is about the average.

Dividend Rate	Volatility							
	10%	20%	30%	40%	50%	60%	70%	80%
0%	0.45	0.49	**0.56**	0.63	0.69	0.75	0.81	0.85
2%	0.28	0.34	**0.40**	0.47	0.54	0.59	0.64	0.68
4%	0.15	0.22	**0.29**	0.35	0.41	0.46	0.51	0.55
6%	0.07	0.14	**0.20**	0.26	0.31	0.36	0.40	0.44
8%	0.02	0.08	**0.14**	0.19	0.24	0.28	0.32	0.35

price and that varies according to a general or industry-specific stock-market index. Although indexed options are attractive because they isolate company performance from broad stock-market trends, they are almost nonexistent, in large part because the accounting rules dissuade companies from even considering them.

For more on indexed options, see Chapter 1, Alfred Rappaport's "New Thinking on How to Link Executive Pay with Performance."

Notes

1. Companies would also be well advised to abandon the practice of "cliff-vesting" the options of executives who are voluntarily departing. In cliff vesting, the vesting periods of all option holdings are collapsed to the present, enabling the executive to exercise all his options the moment he leaves the company. In other words, as soon as an executive's departure date is set, much of his incentive to think long-term disappears.

2. See Stephen F. O'Byrne, "Total Compensation Strategy," *Journal of Applied Corporate Finance* (Summer 1995).

3. For a framework on how to measure the value of nontradable executive (and employee) stock options, see Brian J. Hall and Kevin J. Murphy, "Optimal Exercise Prices for Executive Stock Options," *American Economic Review* (May 2000).

Originally published in March–April 2000
Reprint R00205

When Salaries Aren't Secret

JOHN CASE

Executive Summary

NO ONE SEEMED to think Treece McDavitt was a malevolent employee. "Just mischievous," one person said.

Whatever her motivation, the day before Treece was to leave RightNow!, an off-price women's fashion retailer, the 26-year-old computer wizard accessed HR's files and e-mailed employees' salaries to the entire staff. Now everyone knows what everyone else is making; they are either infuriated that they are making too little or embarrassed that they are making too much. Salary disparities are out there for everyone to see, and CEO Hank Adamson has to do something to smooth things over.

Hank's trusted advisers talk extensively with the CEO about his options, ultimately coming down on two sides. Charlie Herald, vice president of human resources, takes a "You get a lemon, you make lemonade" approach:

keep making the salaries public to ensure fairness and to push employees to higher performance, he advises. Meanwhile, CFO Harriet Duval sees the need for damage control: apologize, clean up the company's compensation system, and continue to keep—or at least *try* to keep—salaries private, she says.

Should Hank side with Charlie or Harriet? Or perhaps find a compromise between their two views? What should he do about this serious salary debacle? Four commentators offer their advice on the problem presented in this fictional case study.

IT HAD ALL HAPPENED so fast. Hunched forward, elbows on the desk, Hank let his chin sink deeper into his hands as he gazed out into the night. Outside, the flowers in the office-park garden looked garish under the orange sodium-vapor lights. Hank didn't notice. He was thinking hard about tomorrow's staff meeting, which had so suddenly been transformed from a celebration into a—well, he wasn't quite sure what. He just knew it wouldn't be pleasant.

Hank Adamson, 48, was chief executive officer of RightNow!, a retail chain specializing in off-price clothing for young, fashion-minded women. Frankly, he had been looking forward to a little celebration. Five years ago, his company had bought out a stodgy, 20-year-old retailer of women's apparel, and Hank had come in to run the place. He renamed it and repositioned it, giving it a hip, edgy style. (*Get Your Clothes Half Off* was the latest slogan, with a racy ad campaign to match.) He invested in rapid growth: RightNow! today had stores in 28 states, with more on the way. Last year, Hank had hired a dozen or so tech-savvy 20-somethings and charged them with creating a killer Web site. Launched just last month, the site was already winning awards and generating substantial business. He'd heard that even the folks in corporate were impressed.

But oh, those 20-somethings. One in particular: Treece McDavitt. Hank had noticed her—you could hardly miss the elaborate tattoos and double eyebrow rings—but he hadn't really known her name. Until yesterday.

"We think it was Treece," Charlie Herald had told him. "It was her last day, and this was her parting shot. Not that we could pin anything on her—she covered her tracks pretty well."

Charlie, RightNow!'s VP of human resources, recounted the story as best as he had been able to piece it together. Treece was hip and edgy herself, a 26-year-old rebel without much of a cause, valuable for her many skills, but not exactly a candidate for Team Player of the Month. Evidently, she had been listening to lunchroom conversations about salaries and had heard all the usual speculation and innuendo about who made what. But where most people just gossiped and let it go, Treece got hot under the collar. She suspected unfairness. She was put out because she and her coworkers knew so little.

"Why shouldn't we know what everyone makes?" she had blurted out one day to her lunchtime companions. "I'll bet there are all kinds of disparities." Everyone laughed and agreed, plunging into irreverent comparisons of what they imagined various managers were paid. One recounted an old IBM commercial in which a malevolent computer hacker e-mails his company's payroll information to all his colleagues.

Treece had smiled. And then the conversation had gone on to other things.

Today, two months later, life was imitating Madison Avenue all too closely. Treece—if it *was* Treece—may have had help from a friend (another recent departure) who worked in HR. Or she may have relied solely on her own considerable computer skills. Whatever, as she herself might have said. No one seemed to think that Treece was a malevolent employee. "Just mischievous," one person said. But it hardly mattered. Even as she made plans to leave the company, she somehow got access to HR's files.

Yesterday was her last day, marked by a small farewell gathering and a few cupcakes. This morning, every RightNow! headquarters employee came in to work to find a camouflaged e-mail waiting on his or her computer. The e-mail bore an attachment, which listed the current salary and most recent bonus of every one of the 165 people who worked in the building.

When Hank had arrived a little after 8:30, Charlie was waiting for him. The vice president got the CEO a cup of black coffee and briefed him. Hank listened but wasn't unduly concerned. "So what?" he had said with a shrug. Everybody talks about money—they always have, always will. Chances are, everybody at the company already has a good idea of what everybody else is making. "Is this really a problem?" he remembered himself asking.

Charlie had looked straight at him. "It's 8:30 in the morning," he said evenly. "I already have four voice mails asking for appointments. I have to think people have something on their minds." Hank asked Charlie to take some soundings around the company, and the two agreed to touch base in the afternoon.

But Hank was talking with store managers all day, and it was five o'clock before Charlie could finally catch him without a phone tucked under his ear. As Charlie walked into Hank's office, Harriet Duval followed. Harriet was RightNow!'s chief financial officer. She and Charlie were Hank's top advisers. As they bustled in, a tune popped into Hank's head and he suppressed a chuckle. Harriet and Charlie always made him think of the line about Iowans from the old show *The Music Man:* they could stand touching noses for a week at a time and never see eye to eye. Harriet and Charlie didn't come from Iowa, so far as Hank knew, but the description did fit—which, of course, was one reason he found them both so valuable.

"Some were teed off because they felt they were earning too little. But others were mortified because now everybody could see they were making more than their buddies."

Charlie looked haggard. "It's worse than we thought," he said. Hank raised an eyebrow; Charlie went on, glumly. "Seems like nobody's been talking about anything else. If you had walked the halls today, you'd have seen little groups all over. People are furious! My assistant Tammy says she's never heard so much griping. And you know those voice mails I mentioned? I must have had a dozen people in my office today, every one of them upset over salaries."

Suddenly reflective, he added: "Funny thing—some were teed off because they felt they were earning too little. You'd expect that, right? But others were mortified because now everybody could see they were making more than their buddies. They wanted to know how to handle it."

Harriet nodded. "For once, I have to agree with Charlie. People are really upset. Heaven knows I've fielded my share of complaints today. At the same time, though, I have to believe it'll blow over in a day or so."

Charlie shook his head. "I don't think so. People get crazy when it comes to money—that's why this company and nearly every other company in the world keep salaries confidential. We're all scared of the reaction. Just today, four or five people actually threatened to walk. One guy even wanted another 30 grand!"

Hank started to ask a question, but Charlie held up a hand.

"Wait," he continued. "You need to know the whole story, and it gets worse. You both know how tight the job market has been recently, especially for marketers experienced in this business. We've had to pay top dollar—

> *"People get crazy when it comes to money—that's why this company and nearly every other company in the world keep salaries confidential."*

and now everybody in the company knows that our four new hires in marketing make more than people who've been around for years." He paused for effect. "And it really doesn't help that three of the four new marketers are men in a department that's almost all female. Can you say 'lawsuit'?"

His listeners winced. "But it isn't just in marketing, it's all over. In the dot-com group, some of those 23-year-olds make north of $50,000. That doesn't look so great to an old-timer in HR who's pulling down $42,000. As for IT, well, don't even go there. We hired that Russian programmer, Arkady, a few years ago at $38,000. He was ecstatic to get the job and is anything but a squeaky wheel when it comes to pay, so he's had only a couple of increases since then. Meanwhile, we bring that young guy Josh in to do the same work. He knows he's good, and he makes sure you know it. He negotiated a high salary when he came on, and he's been relentless in pushing for raises ever since. Now he's making $75,000."

Hank and Harriet sat silent. Harriet reflected uneasily on how her controller—loyal, quiet Edith, who had been at the company more than 20 years—now knew that her salary was less than one-third of Harriet's. Hank thought of Allan, his brother's pal, who was laid off from a much larger apparel chain. To placate his brother, Hank had hired Allan to head up store relations and had matched his big-company salary. It was far more than what Right-Now! would otherwise have paid.

And oh, yes: there was Max, Hank's golfing buddy, who was hired as director of international marketing. Max was a great guy. His wife and Hank's wife were close friends. On the job, he tried hard, but he never got the kind of results a savvier, more aggressive marketer might have achieved. His boss had never given him much in the way of raises, so he earned significantly less than others at his level. Now he—and everyone else—knew it.

Finally Hank spoke: "So we've got a real mess on our hands. And I guess I'm as much to blame as anybody. We've had to add so many people in the last couple of years. I've always told Charlie, 'Get 'em in here. Pay them whatever it takes.'" He thought about mentioning Allan but then decided against it. "And I guess there have been cases where we haven't brought the lower end up fast enough." Charlie nodded tiredly.

"But wait," Harriet said. "Are we really so different from other companies? Everywhere I've worked, there have been pretty big pay disparities. The fact is, you can't really avoid it these days. You have to pay for hot skills— and you have to pay what the market dictates."

"But other companies haven't had their salaries released to the world," Hank said. "And now we're facing this staff meeting tomorrow with 165 teed-off people. Any thoughts about what I should say? Better yet, any thoughts about what we should *do*?"

"Tell them we're going to keep making the salaries public. That we're going to post them." The speaker was Charlie.

Hank and Harriet smiled, ready to laugh at the joke. But Charlie wasn't joking. He was staring at a spot on the floor, his brow furrowed. Suddenly he looked up. "I mean it. I've heard of a couple companies that do this. I think they're on to something."

Now Harriet was incredulous. "Are you nuts? This stuff going public is what's causing all the trouble! A fire breaks out and we're going to douse it with gasoline?"

"Bear with me—the idea isn't as crazy as it sounds." Charlie began to tick off his points on his fingers.

"For starters, consider how hard it is to keep salary information secret anymore. It's all out there in cyberspace, available to anyone smart enough to get it. Think there won't be another Treece?

"Point two. It would keep us honest. We've let our compensation system get out of control. You're right, Harriet: it happens all over. But that's no excuse. Put salaries up on the board, and you can bet the employees will help us make sure they're fair."

Harriet started to argue, but Charlie plowed ahead. "But the real argument is that it helps—heck, it forces—people to understand our business. We've always said we wanted employees to understand our costs and learn to think like businesspeople. Well, here in headquarters our biggest cost is payroll. You should have heard one of the conversations I eavesdropped on today. Somebody was grousing about what we pay the dot-com kids, and two other people jumped all over him. 'Do you know how important those kids are to our future? Do you know what they could earn at one of those IT consulting companies?' Those guys were thinking like CEOs. They shut the complainer right up.

"Besides." Charlie allowed himself a small smile. "You gotta admit that we'd be cutting edge—a sure bet for a story in some big business magazine. Our name in lights."

Harriet rolled her eyes. "Charlie, you aren't thinking straight. You said it yourself—people get crazy over money. Do you really want us to spend all our time explaining to Arkady why he makes so much less than Josh?"

"But that's my point," Charlie retorted. "He shouldn't make so much less. I know—we pay for performance. But is Arkady's performance really only half as valuable as Josh's? If it is, by the way, we should fire him."

"Oh, come off it. You wouldn't even be thinking about their pay if it weren't for the mess we're in right now," Harriet charged.

"Maybe not," Charlie agreed. "But I'm working on the 'you get a lemon, you make lemonade' approach. Sure, we have to say we messed up, we'll be reviewing salaries, the usual blah blah blah. But what if we also say that we think of our employees as partners in the business and that we'll entrust them with the same information every senior manager already has access to—that is, what people make. It'd knock their socks off."

"We're dealing with real people here, and where there are people, there are egos. The problem isn't the disparities that aren't justified; it's the ones that are."

"And make them *very* nervous," Hank interjected.

"Nope. *Yesterday* it would have made them nervous," Charlie replied. "Today they already know the numbers. Now our job is to turn that into something positive."

Harriet shook her head. She had a quick tongue, everybody knew, but she was unusual in her ability to cool off, gather her arguments, then disagree calmly and rationally, without putting people on the defensive. "Charlie, it's a great idea—in theory. But we're dealing with real people here, and where there are people, there are egos. The problem isn't the disparities that *aren't* justified; it's the ones that *are*. We can fix the Arkady-Josh problem. But do we really want to tell Max—sorry, Hank, I know you're friends—that he isn't making more money because he's awkward with clients? Or what about your own assistant Tammy? You know she gets a lot more than anybody else on the support staff, partly because she's always there when some young kid has a problem. She's probably talked a dozen of them out of leaving. If we try to explain that, you can just hear the other AAs." She mimicked a petulant young administrative assistant: "'Well, that's not in *my* job description.'"

The CFO leaned back in her chair, thoughtful. "All those differences in pay—they're the result of stuff you could never talk about out loud. They reflect a hundred judgment calls that every manager makes about every employee every day. You couldn't explain them, so you wouldn't try. Instead you'd run the business like the postal service, paying everybody at a certain grade the same. Or you'd increase everybody's pay with age, like in Japan. Maybe that's okay for the government or for the Japanese, but no business in this hypercompetitive U.S. marketplace could afford it. Our best people wouldn't stand for it."

"Straw man, Harriet." Charlie's tone was earnest. "We're not the post office, and I'm not against differences in pay. I just want reasonable differences." He turned toward Hank. "Look," he said. "This is a people business. We're only as good as our buyers, our marketers, our programmers, even our support staff. And there's this awkward thing about people—they have feelings. People don't care what the market says about what they should be paid; they care what the company says— and they *really* care how much they make compared with the guy in the next office. If they don't feel fairly treated, they get sullen. They do bad things, like leave at five o'clock when there's still work to be done. Or just leave, period."

"You talk like there's some kind of fairness that everybody agrees on," Harriet retorted. "There isn't. People feel it's fair if they earn more than the guy in the next cube. But do you really know anybody who thinks it's fair if they earn less? And now you want to rub their noses in the unfairness? Or have us spend all our time trying to explain it?"

She, too, turned to the CEO. "Hank, Charlie's heart is in the right place, except that it seems to have taken over his brain. Do what he suggests and we're just asking for trouble. At the meeting tomorrow, you should listen sympathetically. You should make all the right noises about conducting a review, examining disparities, and so on. And we should do that, of course; we need to get our compensation system in order. But then we should beef up our computer security so that this never happens again and go about our business. People will continue to gossip for a while. But they'll eventually forget about it."

The two stood up, and Hank thanked them as they left the office. And then he began thinking, and thinking some more, until the sky outside his window turned dark. Charlie's idea? Outlandish, no doubt. But some of his arguments weren't totally crazy, particularly the notion that this would probably happen again sometime. Even if the company didn't post salaries, maybe it could find some middle ground. An employee committee to advise them on salaries? Posting payroll costs by department, with no individual listings? Posting salaries by position, but with no names attached? Hank knew Harriet wouldn't buy any of this. And maybe she was right. Maybe it would all go away.

But maybe they were missing an opportunity, as Charlie believed.

And just how mad were all those employees likely to be at the staff meeting tomorrow? Hank didn't want to make them madder.

Now the night outside was lit only by a crescent moon and those relentless orange lights. The CEO continued to gaze out the window.

What should Hank do about the salary debacle?

Four commentators offer their advice.

VICTOR SIM *is the vice president of total compensation at Prudential Insurance Company of America in Newark, New Jersey.*

I can understand what Hank Adamson's going through because, in a roundabout way, I've been there. My advice to him would be to act but not overreact. Overreacting could create problems that will be difficult to live with later. For one thing, he shouldn't follow

Charlie Herald's advice and publish everyone's salary. That would negatively affect employees' privacy and RightNow!'s ability to compete for talent.

Let me explain why I feel for Hank. As a mutual insurance company, Prudential for years has been required to file with the New York superintendent of insurance the name, title, and compensation of all employees making more than $60,000. The law was designed to disclose the salaries of top executives, as an anticorruption measure to protect policyholders. But over the years, as salaries rose and the law wasn't updated, it in fact applied to a large portion of the workforce.

For a long time, it didn't matter much, even though someone could get all the data from the insurance department. But with the advent of the personal computer and e-mail, it suddenly became much easier to organize and circulate salary information. Then last year, someone posted all the salaries on the Internet. In response, we, along with other insurance companies, asked the insurance department to change its practice by posting the salary for each job but, except in the case of top executives, with no individuals' names attached. Because there are dozens if not hundreds of people in most job categories, anonymity for most people was ensured when the insurance department agreed to our request.

Why did we push for the change? First, there's a personal privacy issue. People who join Prudential don't want their salary information made available to neighbors and friends. In the case of RightNow!, there's no need to add insult to injury for someone like Max, Hank's golfing buddy, who is making less than his colleagues. Second, there's a corporate competition issue. Having the compensation of all employees disclosed in the marketplace makes the company more vulnerable to poaching. Competitors can target individuals, knowing what kinds of salaries they need to offer. The same thing could happen if, as Charlie proposes, RightNow! were to post all names and salaries on a company bulletin board.

Still, Hank needs to acknowledge to his employees that the company's compensation practices need improvement. He should then establish a professionally designed compensation system—one with defined pay grades and salary ranges for each grade. Employees should be involved in the development of the system, contributing ideas on the salary ranges of different jobs and on how merit is actually measured. And the system should be open so that employees know their salary range and have a clear idea of where their job fits into the company's pay structure.

This would allow employees to see how they're being treated relative to others in the company. Without that openness, people end up comparing themselves against the salaries, real or imagined, of other individuals. This raises all kinds of emotional issues. And you're never going to convince everyone that they're being treated fairly in a one-to-one comparison unless you are willing to unearth the nitty-gritty details of each salary decision and air the dirty laundry of every employee.

One frequently cited problem of such a formal pay structure is that it doesn't allow for flexibility in a tight job market, where you typically need to pay a recruitment premium above a job's market value to attract people. One way to avoid paying such a premium, and to maintain the fairness of your salary structure, is to recruit individuals who you believe are ready for the job but have not yet been promoted to an equivalent job in their own companies. For example, a vice president who has been groomed for a senior vice president position at another company, but is waiting for a position to open, may jump at the chance to fill your opening for a senior VP. "Value hiring," like value investing, allows you to pick up bargains, if you will, and pay the market value of the job you are filling.

DENNIS BAKKE *is the CEO of AES Corporation, a $6.7 billion global electricity company based in Arlington, Virginia. He and AES chairman Roger Sant were the subject of the HBR interview "Organizing for Empowerment" (January–February, 1999).*

With all due respect to Charlie, Hank should start by eliminating the entire HR department: compensation should be in the hands of the employees themselves and their leaders, not some staff group. He should eliminate all salary guidelines and publish everyone's pay. And he should require managers to collect input from others before setting an employee's compensation.

To put this in perspective, you must realize that AES has a fairly unconventional approach to managing people. Our electricity plants and distribution companies around the world—and our 53,000 employees—have a lot of autonomy. We don't have any public relations, human resources, or planning departments in the home office or in individual business units. About the only rule we have is that whenever people make important decisions, they have to seek—though not necessarily follow—at least one other employee's advice. We do what we can to encourage an open and honest environment.

At the same time, I have to be honest: 14 years ago, Roger Sant and I suggested to our business managers that they publish people's salaries. I don't think any of them took our advice. The managers basically said that that they didn't want to have to explain salary differences to every single employee. Over the years, some of the younger managers have started sharing more salary information. Although such openness is more difficult for managers, I believe it leads to a healthier work environment. You should indeed have a reason for the salary you set for each individual employee—and be willing and able to justify the differences.

Critics will say that an open-salary system constrains you from paying what is necessary to attract and retain the best people. But perhaps you shouldn't be using money as a weapon in the fight for talent. In AES's early days, I asked people I was recruiting to take a pay cut— not because they didn't deserve the money but because I didn't want money to be the reason people were coming on board. I want them to join because they value an environment where they can use all their gifts and skills without being squelched.

Conversely, we don't have a long vesting period for options because we don't want to set up fences to keep people here one minute longer than they want to be. It's the work environment—not the salary structure—that people ought to be thinking about. Make your company a rewarding and engaging and exciting place to work, and pay issues become far less consequential.

But, you might ask, aren't job categories and guidelines necessary in order to ensure fairness? My feeling is that the entire area of compensation is overmanaged. At AES, we have no salary grades. We don't try to pigeonhole a person's unique abilities and accomplishments into a job category.

Instead, before AES managers set the compensation of direct reports, they solicit feedback from other managers within their group and across the company—and often get the advice of the person whose compensation they are determining. Responses range from "Boy, that seems a little too high" to "Why is this bonus so low?" That shared information gives people a chance to ensure there's some consistency and fairness across and within groups.

I should add that, while most of our businesses still do not publish salaries, we have a plant in Pennsylvania where employees just started setting their own individual salaries. We had tried this in the past and it was a disaster: the good workers set them far too low, and the bad ones set them far too high. But in the most recent case, the group followed our rule of getting advice before making any decision. So the individual employee, before setting his own salary, had to circulate his proposed compensation and get comments from his boss and colleagues. And the plant came in with salaries that were within budget. It's fascinating what you can do without an HR department.

IRA KAY *directs the compensation consulting practice at Watson Wyatt Worldwide, which advises companies on employee benefits, human resources technologies, and human capital management. He is based in New York City.*

The delicate and challenging situation Hank faces could prove to be a big opportunity if he looks at it the right way and understands that his choice is not strictly about compensation policy but about corporate culture. Hank has a chance to embrace a more open culture at RightNow!—one that can have the positive effect of boosting the company's financial performance.

Maintaining a relatively transparent salary structure falls into that category of corporate behaviors—eliminating executive parking spaces, involving lots of people in hiring, limiting the use of titles—that can contribute to a collegial and open work environment. Research we have done at Watson Wyatt indicates that companies with such an environment have higher returns to shareholders because they are typically more innovative and entrepreneurial.

Now that doesn't mean you should reveal everyone's salary, which would undermine the efforts of a fast-growing company like RightNow! to attract talent in a tight job market. If you're going to publish everyone's salary, you need to have internal equity—that is, similar pay for people with similar experience doing similar jobs. And internal equity usually clashes with paying people their external market value. After all, if you hire people from outside the company, you'll typically have to offer them 20% to 25% more than what they currently make—and, in all likelihood, more than what their counterparts in your own company make.

You could change your hiring strategy and promote people solely from within, recruiting them out of college, training them, and moving them up the ranks. But when you're growing rapidly, that isn't possible. Consequently, in the booming economy of the past five years or so, internal equity has given way in most companies to the need to recruit and retain sufficient numbers of the right people. In such a situation, you simply can't have an open-book salary policy.

Harriet Duval is absolutely right: if you have to pay new hires 25% more than people who are already in the same jobs, you can't rub people's faces in that. Nor can you immediately raise everybody's salary to match the new recruits' salaries. You'll simply destroy your margins.

But now that the cat's out of the bag at RightNow!, Hank has to act. A good managerial compromise, and a step toward the open culture that can enhance financial performance, would be to publish the salary ranges—or "bands"—for all of the jobs within the company. Each band will have enough variation to absorb most labor-market or individual-performance differences. High performers who are recruited from the outside might initially be paid above their salary band. But the goal would be to bring everyone within the band, typically by letting the band, and those within it, catch up with the higher paid employees over time.

Publishing salary bands lets people know how their pay compares with others' in the same job and what their jobs are worth relative to others in the company. It lets them know the upside potential of their current job and their career opportunities within the company—all job openings should be disclosed to employees on the corporate intranet—without telling them what everyone else makes. Employees should be treated like adults, with access to as much company information as possible. But some information is just too personal to disclose.

The publication of salary bands is only one of the moves that Hank should make to establish a more open culture. Taken as a whole, these measures would create an environment of trust and collegiality that, interestingly, might ultimately allow RightNow! to adopt Charlie's open-book proposal.

People can build a career at a collegial company in a way that often isn't possible at a place that hires mercenaries from the open market and spits out those who are having short-term performance difficulties. The psychological compensation that comes from working in a supportive environment of long-term commitment might make up for the slightly lower pay that would result from an open-book salary policy.

BRUCE TULGAN *is the author of* Winning the Talent Wars *(W.W. Norton, 2001) and* Managing Generation X *(W.W. Norton, 2000). He is also the founder of Rainmaker Thinking, a management consulting firm based in New Haven, Connecticut.*

Hank is being forced to face the difficult issue of whether to make employee compensation transparent. But what he—and every CEO—should also be considering is something much more radical: whether employees' pay, like contractors' pay, should be negotiated based on the project and the value of the work being done.

Hank must realize the futility of trying to maintain salary secrecy in today's information environment. Countless Web sites let employees examine salary surveys throughout entire industries. Individuals can also test their own true market value through the now common practice of continuous job shopping. What's more, this job shopping can be done in a low-risk manner at job-search and talent-auction Web sites.

Charlie is right to consider that another employee down the road might access compensation data and repeat Treece's e-mail mischief. But there's a more important point: top executives, supervisors, HR professionals, and accounting people have always been in the know about individuals' salaries. And people today—especially those in the workforce born after 1963, Generation X and

Generation Y—are much more open about sharing and comparing pay information with their peers. With so much information swirling around today's business landscape, more speculation about compensation will occur up and down the corporate ladder. Surely, accurate information is more constructive than speculation.

Indeed, the growing availability of accurate information about the real value of workers' skills, abilities, and output is critical to making the overall labor market more fluid and more efficient. That larger economic trend is too powerful for any one employer to overlook. Employers should not buck the trend.

Without wage transparency, market pressures cannot work their true magic and ensure that compensation reflects real value. We see this in the case study. One of the main reasons that Hank and Harriet are worried about the public disclosure of salaries is that they know their company's compensation system is not entirely performance based. One solution is to make the system more rigorous so that it reflects real value.

Harriet says that even a fair system will seem unfair by employees whose feelings may be hurt. This concern is archaic and paternalistic. Employees must be sophisticated enough to understand their manager's reasoning, to negotiate on their own behalf, and to make decisions about the relative fairness of salaries. True, some employees won't succeed with that degree of pressure. But smart companies are looking for employees who respond to that pressure by becoming more valuable. And most employees won't resent compensation differentials based on ongoing transparent pay-for-performance negotiations.

Every step of the way, managers must clearly define each employee's objectives and tie rewards directly to meeting those objectives. The most important transparency factor is not whether employees know what others earn, but rather that all of them know exactly why they earn what they do and what they need to do to earn more.

Harriet and Hank make an important point when they say that intangible factors require managers to be subjective when evaluating employee performance. That's why the ongoing negotiation process is so important. The worth of one employee's work today is whatever the day's negotiation yields. That kind of real market pressure on both employers and employees will drive worker productivity through the roof.

Managers at RightNow! will have to roll up their sleeves, negotiate short-term pay-for-performance deals with every employee on every project, measure every individual's performance every day, and keep good contemporaneous records. Harriet is dead right: it's going to be an extremely high maintenance system for managers. But if you want high productivity, you have to accept high maintenance.

Originally published in May 2001
Reprint R0105A

Six Dangerous Myths About Pay

JEFFREY PFEFFER

Executive Summary

EVERY DAY, EXECUTIVES make decisions about pay, and they do so in a landscape that's shifting. As more and more companies base less of their compensation on straight salary and look to other financial options, managers are bombarded with advice about the best approaches to take.

Unfortunately, much of that advice is wrong. Indeed, much of the conventional wisdom and public discussion about pay today is misleading, incorrect, or both. The result is that businesspeople are adopting wrongheaded notions about how to pay people and why. In particular, they are subscribing to six dangerous myths about pay.

- Myth #1: labor rates are the same as labor costs.

- Myth #2: cutting labor rates will lower labor costs.

- Myth #3: labor costs represent a large portion of a company's total costs.

- Myth #4: keeping labor costs low creates a potent and sustainable competitive edge.
- Myth #5: individual incentive pay improves performance.
- Myth # 6: people work primarily for the money.

The author explains why these myths are so pervasive, shows where they go wrong, and suggests how leaders might think more productively about compensation.

With increasing frequency, the author says, he sees managers harming their organizations by buying into—and acting on—these myths. Those that do, he warns, are probably doomed to endless tinkering with pay that at the end of the day will accomplish little but cost a lot.

Consider two groups of steel minimills. One group pays an average hourly wage of $18.07. The second pays an average of $21.52 an hour. Assuming that other direct-employment costs, such as benefits, are the same for the two groups, which group has the higher labor costs?

An airline is seeking to compete in the low-cost, low-frills segment of the U.S. market where, for obvious reasons, labor productivity and efficiency are crucial for competitive success. The company pays virtually no one on the basis of individual merit or performance. Does it stand a chance of success?

A company that operates in an intensely competitive segment of the software industry does not pay its sales force on commission. Nor does it pay individual bonuses or offer stock options or phantom stock, common incentives in an industry heavily dependent on attracting and retaining scarce programming talent. Would you invest in this company?

Every day, organizational leaders confront decisions about pay. Should they adjust the company's compensation system to encourage some set of behaviors? Should they retain consultants to help them implement a performance-based pay system? How large a raise should they authorize?

In general terms, these kinds of questions come down to four decisions about compensation:

- how much to pay employees;

- how much emphasis to place on financial compensation as a part of the total reward system;

- how much emphasis to place on attempting to hold down the rate of pay; and

- whether to implement a system of individual incentives to reward differences in performance and productivity and, if so, how much emphasis to place on these incentives.

For leaders, there can be no delegation of these matters. Everyone knows decisions about pay are important. For one thing, they help establish a company's culture by rewarding the business activities, behaviors, and values that senior managers hold dear. Senior management at Quantum, the disk drive manufacturer in Milpitas, California, for example, demonstrates its commitment to teamwork by placing all employees, from the CEO to hourly workers, on the same bonus plan, tracking everyone by the same measure—in this case, return on total capital.

Managers are bombarded with advice about pay. Unfortunately, much of that advice is wrong.

Truth and Consequences:
The Six Dangerous Myths About Compensation

Myth	Reality
1. Labor rates and labor costs are the same thing.	1. They are not, and confusing them leads to a host of managerial missteps. For the record, labor rates are straight wages divided by time—a Wal-Mart cashier earns $5.15 an hour, a Wall Street attorney $2,000 a day. Labor costs are a calculation of how much a company pays its people and how much they produce. Thus German factory workers may be paid at a rate of $30 an hour and Indonesians $3, but the workers' relative costs will reflect how many widgets are produced in the same period of time.
2. You can lower your labor costs by cutting labor rates.	2. When managers buy into the myth that labor rates and labor costs are the same thing, they usually fall for this myth as well. Once again, then, labor costs are a function of labor rates and productivity. To lower labor costs, you need to address *both*. Indeed, sometimes lowering labor rates increases labor costs.
3. Labor costs constitute a significant proportion of total costs.	3. This is true—but only sometimes. Labor costs as a proportion of total costs vary widely by industry and company. Yet many executives assume labor costs are the biggest expense on their income statement. In fact, labor costs are only the most immediately malleable expense.
4. Low labor costs are a potent and sustainable competitive weapon.	4. In fact, labor costs are perhaps the most slippery and least sustainable way to compete. Better to achieve competitive advantage through quality; through customer service; through product, process, or service innovation; or through technology leadership. It is much more difficult to imitate these sources of competitive advantage than to merely cut costs.
5. Individual incentive pay improves performance.	5. Individual incentive pay, in reality, undermines performance—of both the individual and the organization. Many studies strongly suggest that this form of reward undermines teamwork, encourages a short-term focus, and leads people to believe that pay is not related to performance at all but to having the "right" relationships and an ingratiating personality.
6. People work for money.	6. People do work for money—but they work even more for meaning in their lives. In fact, they work to have fun. Companies that ignore this fact are essentially bribing their employees and will pay the price in a lack of loyalty and commitment.

Compensation is also a concept and practice very much in flux. Compensation is becoming more variable as companies base a greater proportion of it on stock options and bonuses and a smaller proportion on base salary, not only for executives but also for people further and further down the hierarchy. As managers make organization-defining decisions about pay systems, they do so in a shifting landscape while being bombarded with advice about the best routes to stable ground.

Unfortunately, much of that advice is wrong. Indeed, much of the conventional wisdom and public discussion about pay today is misleading, incorrect, or sometimes both at the same time. The result is that businesspeople end up adopting wrongheaded notions about how to pay people and why. They believe in six dangerous myths about pay—fictions about compensation that have somehow come to be seen as the truth. (See "Truth and Consequences: The Six Dangerous Myths about Compensation.")

Do you think you have managed to avoid these myths? Let's see how you answered the three questions that open this article. If you said the second set of steel minimills had higher labor costs, you fell into the common trap of confusing labor *rates* with labor *costs*. That is Myth #1: that labor rates and labor costs are the same thing. But how different they really are. The second set of minimills paid its workers at a rate of $3.45 an hour more than the first. But according to data collected by Fairfield University Professor Jeffrey Arthur, its labor costs were much lower because the productivity of the mills was higher. The second set of mills actually required 34% fewer labor hours to produce a ton of steel than the first set and also generated 63%

less scrap. The second set of mills could have raised workers' pay rate by 19% and still had lower labor costs.

Connected to the first myth are three more myths that draw on the same logic. When managers believe that labor costs and labor rates are the same thing, they also tend to believe that they can cut labor costs by cutting labor rates. That's Myth #2. Again, this leaves out the important matter of productivity. I may replace my $2,000-a-week engineers with ones that earn $500 a week, but my costs may skyrocket because the new, lower-paid employees are inexperienced, slow, and less capable. In that case, I would have increased my costs by cutting my rates.

Managers who mix up labor rates and labor costs also tend to accept Myth #3: that labor costs are a significant portion of total costs. Sometimes, that's true. It is, for example, at accounting and consulting firms. But the ratio of labor costs to total costs varies widely in different industries and companies. And even where it is true, it's not as important as many managers believe. Those who swallow Myth #4—that low labor costs are a potent competitive strategy—may neglect other, more effective ways of competing, such as through quality, service, delivery, and innovation. In reality, low labor costs are a slippery way to compete and perhaps the least sustainable competitive advantage there is.

Those of you who believed that the airline trying to compete in the low-cost, low-frills segment of the U.S. market would not succeed without using individual incentives succumbed to Myth #5: that the most effective way to motivate people to work productively is through individual incentive compensation. But Southwest Airlines has never used such a system, and it is the cost *and* productivity leader in its industry. Southwest is not alone, but still it takes smart, informed managers to buck the trend of offering individual rewards.

Would you have invested in the computer software company that didn't offer its people bonuses, stock options, or other financial incentives that could make them millionaires? You should have because it has succeeded mightily, growing over the past 21 years at a compound annual rate of more than 25%. The company is the SAS Institute of Cary, North Carolina. Today it is the largest privately held company in the software industry, with 1997 revenues of some $750 million.

Rather than emphasize pay, SAS has achieved an unbelievably low turnover rate below 4%—in an industry where the norm is closer to 20%—by offering intellectually engaging work; a family-friendly environment that features exceptional benefits; and the opportunity to work with fun, interesting people using state-of-the-art equipment.

In short, SAS has escaped Myth #6: that people work primarily for money. SAS, operating under the opposite assumption, demonstrates otherwise. In the last three years, the company has lost *none* of its 20 North American district sales managers. How many software companies do you know could make that statement, even about the last three months?

Every day, I see managers harming their organizations by believing in these myths about pay. What I want to do in these following pages is explore some factors that help account for why the myths are so pervasive, present some evidence to disprove their underlying assumptions, and suggest how leaders might think more productively and usefully about the important issue of pay practices in their organizations.

Why the Myths Exist

On October 10, 1997, the *Wall Street Journal* published an article expressing surprise that a "contrarian Motorola" had chosen to build a plant in Germany to make cellular phones despite the notoriously high "cost" of German labor. The *Journal* is not alone in framing business decisions about pay in this way. The *Economist* has also written articles about high German labor "costs," citing as evidence labor rates (including fringe benefits) of more than $30 per hour.

The semantic confusion of labor rates with labor costs, endemic in business journalism and everyday discussion, leads managers to see the two as equivalent. And when the two seem equivalent, the associated myths about labor costs seem to make sense, too. But, of course, labor rates and labor costs simply aren't the same thing. A labor rate is total salary divided by time worked. But labor costs take productivity into account. That's how the second set of minimills managed to have lower labor costs than the mills with the lower wages. They made more steel, and they made it faster and better.

Another reason why the confusion over costs and rates persists is that labor rates are a convenient target for managers who want to make an impact. Labor rates are highly visible, and it's easy to compare the rates you pay with those paid by your competitors or with those paid in other parts of the world. In addition, labor rates often appear to be a company's most malleable financial variable. It seems a lot quicker and easier to cut wages than to control costs in other ways, like reconfiguring manufacturing processes, changing corporate culture, or altering product design. Because labor costs appear to be the lever closest at hand, managers mistakenly assume it is the one that has the most leverage.

For the myths that individual incentive pay drives creativity and productivity, and that people are primarily motivated by money, we have economic theory to blame. More specifically, we can blame the economic model of human behavior widely taught in business schools and held to be true in the popular press. This model presumes that behavior is rational—driven by the best information available at the time and designed to maximize the individual's self-interest. According to this model, people take jobs and decide how much effort to expend in those jobs based on their expected financial return. If pay is not contingent on performance, the theory goes, individuals will not devote sufficient attention and energy to their jobs.

Additional problems arise from such popular economic concepts as agency theory (which contends that there are differences in preference and perspective between owners and those who work for them) and transaction-cost economics (which tries to identify which transactions are best organized by markets and which by hierarchies). Embedded in both concepts is the idea that individuals not only pursue self-interest but do so on occasion with guile and opportunism. Thus agency theory suggests that employees have different objectives than their employers and, moreover, have opportunities to misrepresent information and divert resources to their personal use. Transaction-cost theory suggests that people will make false or empty threats and promises to get better deals from one another.

All of these economic models portray work as hard and aversive—implying that the only way people can be induced to work is through some combination of rewards and sanctions. As professor James N. Baron of Stanford Business School has written, "The image of workers in these models is somewhat akin to Newton's first law of motion: employees remain in a state of rest unless compelled to change that state by a stronger force impressed upon them—namely, an optimal labor contract."

Similarly, the language of economics is filled with terms such as *shirking* and *free riding*. Language is powerful, and as Robert Frank, himself an economist, has noted, theories of human behavior become self-fulfilling. We act on the basis of these theories, and through our own actions produce in others the behavior we expect. If we believe people will work hard only if specifically rewarded for doing so, we will provide contingent rewards and thereby condition people to work only when they are rewarded. If we expect people to be untrustworthy, we will closely monitor and control them and by doing so will signal that they can't be trusted—an expectation that they will most likely confirm for us.

So self-reinforcing are these ideas that you almost have to avoid mainstream business to get away from them. Perhaps that's why several companies known to be strongly committed to managing through trust, mutual respect, and true decentralization—such as AES Corporation, Lincoln Electric, the Men's Wearhouse, the SAS Institute, ServiceMaster, Southwest Airlines, and Whole Foods Market—tend to avoid recruiting at conventional business schools.

It's simpler for managers to tinker with compensation than to change the company's culture.

There's one last factor that helps perpetuate all these myths: the compensation-consulting industry. Unfortunately, that industry has a number of perverse incentives to keep these myths alive.

First, although some of these consulting firms have recently broadened their practices, compensation remains their bread and butter. Suggesting that an organization's performance can be improved in some way other than by tinkering with the pay system may be empirically correct but is probably too selfless a behavior to expect from these firms.

Second, if it's simpler for managers to tinker with the compensation system than to change an organization's culture, the way work is organized, and the level of trust and respect the system displays, it's even easier for consultants. Thus both the compensation consultants and their clients are tempted by the apparent speed and ease with which reward-system solutions can be implemented.

Third, to the extent that changes in pay systems bring their own new predicaments, the consultants will continue to have work solving the problems that the tinkering has caused in the first place.

From Myth to Reality: A Look at the Evidence

The media are filled with accounts of companies attempting to reduce their labor costs by laying off people, moving production to places where labor rates are lower, freezing wages, or some combination of the above. In the early 1990s, for instance, Ford decided not to award merit raises to its white-collar workers as part of a new cost-cutting program. And in 1997, General Motors endured a series of highly publicized strikes over the issue of outsourcing. GM wanted to move more of its work to nonunion, presumably lower-wage, suppliers to reduce its labor costs and become more profitable.

Ford's and GM's decisions were driven by the myths that labor rates and labor costs are the same thing, and that labor costs constitute a significant portion of total costs. Yet hard evidence to support those contentions is slim. New United Motor Manufacturing, the joint venture between Toyota and General Motors based in Fremont, California, paid the highest wage in the automobile industry when it began operations in the mid-1980s, and it also offered a guarantee of secure employment. With productivity some 50% higher than at comparable GM plants, the venture could afford to pay 10% more and still come out ahead.

Yet General Motors apparently did not learn the lesson that what matters is not pay rate but productivity. In May 1996, as GM was preparing to confront the union over the issue of outsourcing, the "Harbour Report," the automobile industry's bible of comparative efficiency, published some interesting data suggesting that General Motors' problems had little to do with labor rates. As reported in the *Wall Street Journal* at the time, the report showed that it took General Motors some 46 hours to assemble a car, while it took Ford just 37.92 hours, Toyota 29.44, and Nissan only 27.36. As a way of attacking cost problems, officials at General Motors should have asked why they needed 21% more hours than Ford to accomplish the same thing or why GM was some 68% less efficient than Nissan.

For more evidence of how reality really looks, consider the machine tool industry. Many of its senior managers have been particularly concerned with low-cost foreign competition, believing that the cost advantage has come from the lower labor rates available offshore. But for machine tool companies that stop fixating on labor rates and focus instead on their overall management system and manufacturing processes, there are great potential returns. Cincinnati Milacron, a company that had virtually surrendered the market for low-end machine tools to Asian competitors by the mid-1980s, overhauled its assembly process, abolished its stockroom, and reduced job categories from seven to one. Without any capital investment, those changes in the production *process* reduced labor hours by 50%, and the company's productivity is now higher than its competitors' in Taiwan.

Even U.S. apparel manufacturers lend support to the argument that labor costs are not the be-all and end-all of profitability. Companies in this industry are generally obsessed with finding places where hourly wages are low. But the cost of direct labor needed to manufacture a pair of jeans is actually only about 15% of total costs, and even the direct labor involved in producing a man's suit is only about $12.50.[1]

Compelling evidence also exists to dispute the myth that competing on labor costs will create any sustainable advantage. Let's start close to home. One day, I arrived at a large discount store with a shopping list. Having the good fortune to actually find a sales associate, I asked him where I could locate the first item on my list. "I don't know," he replied. He gave a similar reply when queried about the second item. A glance at the long list I was holding brought the confession that because of high employee turnover, the young man had been in the store only a few hours himself. What is that employee worth to the store? Not only can't he sell the merchandise, he can't even find it! Needless to say, I wasn't able to purchase everything on my list because I got tired of looking and gave up. And I haven't returned since. Companies that compete on cost alone eventually bump into consumers like me. It's no accident that Wal-Mart combines its low-price strategy with friendly staff members greeting people at the door and works assiduously to keep turnover low.

Another example of a company that understands the limits of competing solely on labor costs is the Men's Wearhouse, the enormously successful off-price retailer of tailored men's clothing. The company operates in a fiercely competitive industry in which growth is possible primarily by taking sales from competitors, and price wars are intense. Still, less than 15% of the company's staff is part-time, wages are higher than the industry average, and the company engages in extensive training. All these policies defy conventional wisdom for the retailing industry. But the issue isn't what the Men's Wearhouse's employees cost, it's what they can do: sell very effectively because of their product knowledge and sales skills. Moreover, by keeping inventory losses and employee turnover low, the company saves money on shrinkage and hiring. Companies that miss this point—that costs, particularly labor costs, aren't everything—often overlook ways of succeeding that competitors can't readily copy.

Evidence also exists that challenges the myth about the effectiveness of individual incentives. This evidence, however, has done little to stem the tide of individual merit pay. A survey of the pay practices of the *Fortune* 1,000 reported that between 1987 and 1993, the proportion of companies using individual incentives for at least 20% of their workforce increased from 38% to 50% while the proportion of companies using profit sharing—a more collective reward—decreased from 45% to 43%. Between 1981 and 1990, the proportion of retail salespeople that were paid solely on straight salary, with no commission, declined from 21% to 7%. And this trend toward individual incentive compensation is not confined to the United States. A study of pay practices at plants in the United Kingdom reported that the proportion using some form of merit pay had increased every year since 1986 such that by 1990 it had reached 50%.[2]

Despite the evident popularity of this practice, the problems with individual merit pay are numerous and well documented. It has been shown to undermine teamwork, encourage employees to focus on the short term, and lead people to link compensation to political skills and ingratiating personalities rather than to performance. Indeed, those are among the reasons why W. Edwards Deming and other quality experts have argued strongly against using such schemes.

Consider the results of several studies. One carefully designed study of a performance-contingent pay plan at 20 Social Security Administration offices found that merit pay had no effect on office performance. Even though the merit pay plan was contingent on a number of objective indicators, such as the time taken to settle claims and the accuracy of claims processing, employees exhibited no difference in performance after the merit pay plan was introduced as part of a reform of civil service pay practices. Contrast that study with another that examined the elimination of a piecework system and its replacement by a more group-oriented compensation

Most merit-pay systems share two attributes: they absorb vast amounts of management time and make everybody unhappy.

system at a manufacturer of exhaust system components. There, grievances decreased, product quality increased almost tenfold, and perceptions of teamwork and concern for performance all improved.[3]

Surveys conducted by various consulting companies that specialize in management and compensation also reveal the problems and dissatisfaction with individual merit pay. For instance, a study by the consulting firm William M. Mercer reported that 73% of the responding companies had made major changes to their performance-management plans in the preceding two years, as they experimented with different ways to tie pay to individual performance. But 47% reported that their employees found the systems neither fair nor sensible, and 51% of the employees said that the performance-management system provided little value to the company. No wonder Mercer concluded that most individual merit or performance-based pay plans share two attributes: they absorb vast amounts of management time and resources, and they make everybody unhappy.

One concern about paying on a more group-oriented basis is the so-called free-rider problem, the worry that people will not work hard because they know that if rewards are based on collective performance and their colleagues make the effort, they will share in those rewards regardless of the level of their individual efforts. But there are two reasons why organizations should not be reluctant to design such collective pay systems.

First, much to the surprise of people who have spent too much time reading economics, empirical evidence from numerous studies indicates that the extent of free riding is quite modest. For instance, one comprehensive review reported that "under the conditions described by the theory as leading to free riding, people often cooperate instead."[4]

Second, individuals do not make decisions about how much effort to expend in a social vacuum; they are influenced by peer pressure and the social relations they have with their workmates. This social influence is potent, and although it may be somewhat stronger in smaller groups, it can be a force mitigating against free riding even in large organizations. As one might expect, then, there is evidence that organizations paying on a more collective basis, such as through profit sharing or gain sharing, outperform those that don't.

Sometimes, individual pay schemes go so far as to affect customers. Sears was forced to eliminate a commission system at its automobile repair stores in California when officials found widespread evidence of consumer fraud. Employees, anxious to meet quotas and earn commissions on repair sales, were selling unneeded services to unsuspecting customers. Similarly, in 1992, the *Wall Street Journal* reported that Highland Superstores, an electronics and appliance retailer, eliminated commissions because they had encouraged such aggressive behavior on the part of salespeople that customers were alienated.

Enchantment with individual merit pay reflects not only the belief that people won't work effectively if they are not rewarded for their individual efforts but also the related view that the road to solving organizational problems is largely paved with adjustments to pay and measurement practices. Consider again the data from the Mercer survey: nearly three-quarters of all the companies surveyed had made *major* changes to their pay plans in just the past two years. That's tinkering on a grand scale. Or take the case of Air Products and Chemicals of Allentown, Pennsylvania. When on October 23, 1996, the company reported mediocre sales and profits, the stock price declined from the low $60s to the high $50s. Eight days later, the company announced a new set of management-compensation and stock-ownership initiatives designed to reassure Wall Street that management cared about its shareholders and was demonstrating that concern by changing compensation arrangements. The results were dramatic. On the day of the announcement, the stock price went up 1 1/4 points, and the next day it rose an additional 4 3/4 points. By November 29, Air Products' stock had gone up more than 15%. According to Value Line, this rise was an enthusiastic reaction by investors to the new compensation system. No wonder managers are so tempted to tamper with pay practices!

But as Bill Strusz, director of corporate industrial relations at Xerox in Rochester, New York, has said, if managers seeking to improve performance or solve organizational problems use compensation as the only lever, they will get two results: nothing will happen, and they will spend a lot of money. That's because people want more out of their jobs than just money. Numerous surveys—even of second-year M.B.A. students, who frequently graduate with large amounts of debt—indicate that money is far from the most important factor in choosing a job or remaining in one.

Why has the SAS Institute had such low turnover in the software industry despite its tight labor market? When asked this question, employees said they were motivated by SAS's unique perks—plentiful opportunities to work with the latest and most up-to-date equipment and the ease with which they could move back and forth between being a manager and being an individual contributor. They also cited how much

I would not necessarily say that external rewards backfire, but they do create their own problems.

variety there was in the projects they worked on, how intelligent and nice the people they worked with were, and how much the organization cared for and appreciated them. Of course, SAS pays competitive salaries, but in an industry in which people have the opportunity to become millionaires through stock options by moving to a competitor, the key to retention is SAS's culture, not its monetary rewards.

People seek, in a phrase, an enjoyable work environment. That's what AES, the Men's Wearhouse, SAS, and Southwest have in common. One of the core values at each company is *fun*. When a colleague and I wrote a business school case on Southwest, we asked some of the employees, a number of whom had been offered much more money to work elsewhere, why they stayed. The answer we heard repeatedly was that they knew what the other environments were like, and they would rather be at a place, as one employee put it, where *work* is not a four-letter word. This doesn't mean work has to be easy. As an AES employee noted, fun means working in a place where people can use their gifts and skills and can work with others in an atmosphere of mutual respect.

There is a great body of literature on the effect of large external rewards on individuals' intrinsic motivation. The literature argues that extrinsic rewards diminish intrinsic motivation and, moreover, that large extrinsic rewards can actually decrease performance in tasks that require creativity and innovation. I would not necessarily go so far as to say that external rewards backfire, but they certainly create their own problems. First, people receiving such rewards can reduce their own motivation through a trick of self-perception, figuring, "I must not like the job if I have to be paid so much to do it" or "I make so much, I must be doing it for the money." Second, they undermine their own loyalty or performance by reacting against a sense of being controlled, thinking something like, "I will show the company that I can't be controlled just through money."

But most important, to my mind, is the logic in the idea that any organization believing it can solve its attraction, retention, and motivation problems solely by its compensation system is probably not spending as much time and effort as it should on the work environment—on defining its jobs, on creating its culture, and on making work fun and meaningful. It is a question of time and attention, of scarce managerial resources. The time and attention spent managing the reward system are not available to devote to other aspects of the work environment that in the end may be much more critical to success.

Some Advice About Pay

Since I have traipsed you through a discussion of what's wrong with the way most companies approach compensation, let me now offer some advice about how to get it right.

The first, and perhaps most obvious, suggestion is that managers would do well to keep the difference between labor rates and labor costs straight. In doing so, remember that only labor costs—and not labor rates—are the basis for competition, and that labor costs may not be a major component of total costs. In any event, managers should remember that the issue is not just what you pay people, but also what they produce.

If you could reliably measure and reward individual contributions, organizations wouldn't be needed.

To combat the myth about the effectiveness of individual performance pay, managers should see what happens when they include a large dose of collective rewards in their employees' compensation package. The more aggregated the unit used to measure performance, the more reliably performance can be assessed. One can tell pretty accurately how well an organization, or even a subunit, has done with respect to sales, profits, quality, productivity, and the like. Trying to parcel out who, specifically, was responsible for exactly how much of that productivity, quality, or sales is frequently much more difficult or even impossible. As Herbert Simon, the Nobel-prize-winning economist, has recognized, people in organizations are interdependent, and therefore organizational results are the consequence of collective behavior and performance. If you could reliably and easily measure and reward individual contributions, you probably would not need an organization at all as everyone would enter markets solely as individuals.

In the typical individual-based merit pay system, the boss works with a raise budget that's some percentage of the total salary budget for the unit. It's inherently a zero-sum process: the more I get in my raise, the less is left for my colleagues. So the worse my workmates perform, the happier I am because I know I will look better by comparison. A similar dynamic can occur across organizational units in which competition for a fixed bonus pool discourages people from sharing best practices and learning from employees in other parts of the organization. In November 1995, for example, *Fortune* magazine reported that at Lantech, a manufacturer of packaging machinery in Louisville, Kentucky, individual incentives caused such intense rivalry that the chairman of the company, Pat Lancaster, said, "I was spending 95% of my time on conflict resolution instead of on how to serve our customers."

Managers can fight the myth that people are primarily motivated by money by de-emphasizing pay and not portraying it as the main thing you get from working at a particular company. How? Consider the example of Tandem Computer which, in the years before it was acquired by Compaq, would not even tell you your salary before expecting you to accept a job. If you asked, you would be told that Tandem paid good, competitive salaries. The company had a simple philosophy—if you came for money, you would leave for money, and Tandem wanted employees who were there because they liked the work, the culture, and the people, not something—money— that every company could offer. Emphasizing pay as the primary reward encourages people to come and to stay for the wrong reasons. AES, a global independent power producer in Arlington, Virginia, has a relatively short vesting period for retirement-plan contributions and tries not to pay the highest salaries for jobs in its local labor market. By so doing, it seeks to ensure that people are not locked into working at a place where they don't want to be simply for the money.

Managers must also recognize that pay has substantive and symbolic components. In signaling what and who in the organization is valued, pay both reflects and helps determine the organization's culture. Therefore, managers must make sure that the messages sent by pay practices are intended. Talking about teamwork and cooperation and then not having a group-based component to the pay system matters because paying solely on an individual basis signals what the organization believes is actually important—individual behavior and performance. Talking about the importance of *all* people in the organization and then paying some disproportionately more than others belies that message. One need not go to the extreme of Whole Foods Market, which pays no one more than eight times the average company salary (the result being close to $1 billion in sales at a company where the CEO makes less than $200,000 a year). But paying large executive bonuses while laying off people and asking for wage freezes, as General Motors did in the 1980s, may not send the right message, either. When Southwest Airlines asked its pilots for a five-year wage freeze, CEO Herb Kelleher voluntarily asked the compensation committee to freeze his salary for at least four years as well. The message of shared, common fate is powerful in an organization truly seeking to build a culture of teamwork.

Making pay practices public also sends a powerful symbolic message. Some organizations reveal pay distributions by position or level. A few organizations, such as Whole Foods Market, actually make data on individual pay available to all members who are interested. Other organizations try to maintain a high level of secrecy about pay. What message do those organizations send? Keeping salaries secret suggests that the organization has something to hide or that it doesn't trust its people with the information. Moreover, keeping things secret just encourages people to uncover the secrets—if something is worth hiding, it must be important and interesting enough to expend effort discovering. Pay systems that are more open and transparent send a positive message about the equity of the system and the trust that the company places in its people.

Managers should also consider using other methods besides pay to signal company values and focus behavior. The head of North American sales and operations for the SAS Institute has a useful perspective on this issue. He didn't think he was smart enough to design an incentive system that couldn't be gamed. Instead of using the pay system to signal what was important, he and other SAS managers simply told people what was important for the company and why. That resulted in much more nuanced and rapid changes in behavior because the company didn't have to change the compensation system every time business priorities altered a little. What a novel idea—actually talking to people about what is important and why, rather than trying to send some subtle signals through the compensation system!

Perhaps most important, leaders must come to see pay for what it is: just one element in a set of management practices that can either build or reduce commitment, teamwork, and performance. Thus my final piece of advice about pay is to make sure that pay practices are congruent with other management practices and reinforce rather than oppose their effects.

Breaking with Convention to Break the Myths

Many organizations devote enormous amounts of time and energy to their pay systems, but people, from senior managers to hourly workers, remain unhappy with them. Organizations are trapped in unproductive ways of approaching pay, which they find difficult to escape. The reason, I would suggest, is that

Pay cannot substitute for a working environment high on trust, fun, and meaningful work.

people are afraid to challenge the myths about compensation. It's easier and less controversial to see what everyone else is doing and then to do the same. In fact, when I talk to executives at companies about installing pay systems that actually work, I usually hear, "But that's different from what most other companies are saying and doing."

It must certainly be the case that a company cannot earn "abnormal" returns by following the crowd. That's true about marketplace strategies, and it's true about compensation. Companies that are truly exceptional are not trapped by convention but instead see and pursue a better business model.

Companies that have successfully transcended the myths about pay know that pay cannot substitute for a working environment high on trust, fun, and meaningful work. They also know that it is more important to worry about what people do than what they cost, and that zero-sum pay plans can set off internal competition that makes learning from others, teamwork, and cross-functional cooperation a dream rather than the way the place works on an everyday basis.

There is an interesting paradox in achieving high organizational performance through innovative pay practices—if it were easy to do, it wouldn't provide as much competitive leverage as it actually does. So while I can review the logic and evidence and offer some alternative ways of thinking about pay, it is the job of leaders to exercise both the judgment and the courage necessary to break with common practice. Those who do will develop organizations in which pay practices actually contribute rather than detract from building high-performance management systems. Those who are stuck in the past are probably doomed to endless tinkering with pay; at the end of the day, they won't have accomplished much, but they will have expended a lot of time and money doing it.

Notes

1. John T. Dunlop and David Weil, "Diffusion and Performance of Modular Production in the U.S. Apparel Industry," *Industrial Relations*, July 1996, p. 337.

2. For the survey of the pay practices of *Fortune* 1,000 companies, see Gerald E. Ledford, Jr., Edward E. Lawler III, and Susan A. Mohrman, "Reward Innovations in *Fortune* 1,000 Companies," *Compensation and Benefits Review*, April 1995, p. 76; for the salary and commission data, see Gregory A. Patterson, "Distressed Shoppers, Disaffected Workers Prompt Stores to Alter Sales Commissions," the *Wall Street Journal*, July 1, 1992, p. B1; for the study of U.K. pay practices, see Stephen Wood, "High Commitment Management and Payment Systems," *Journal of Management Studies*, January 1996, p. 53.

3. For the Social Security Administration study, see Jone L. Pearce, William B. Stevenson, and James L. Perry, "Managerial Compensation Based on Organizational Performance: A Time Series Analysis of the Effects of Merit Pay," *Academy of Management Journal*, June 1985, p. 261; for the study of group-oriented compensation, see Larry Hatcher and Timothy L. Ross, "From Individual Incentives to an Organization-Wide Gainsharing Plan: Effects on Teamwork and Product Quality," *Journal of Organizational Behavior*, May 1991, p. 169.

4. Gerald Marwell, "Altruism and the Problem of Collective Action," in V.J. Derlega and J. Grzelak, eds., *Cooperation and Helping Behavior: Theories and Research* (New York Academic Press, 1982), p. 208.

Originally published in May–June 1998
Reprint 98309

Growing Pains

Executive Summary

CYRUS MAHER, CEO of Waterway Industries, thinks he
may be facing a human resources problem. Lee Carter is
a relatively new employee whose high-powered sales
ability has rocketed Maher's sleepy canoe company
into unprecedented growth. But Maher has overheard
Carter discussing a new job that would offer equity, and
he fears her defection is imminent.

Maher has begun to reconsider his employees' compensation arrangements, particularly Carter's. As he con-
sults with his banker and with advisers in the industry, he
begins to realize that the easygoing culture he created
at Waterway may have changed for good.

His employees are outdoor types who clear the
building by 4 P.M. on a nice day. They have good
morale and love designing and making the canoes and
kayaks that delight like-minded customers. But now

167

Waterway is in a higher-stakes game, and even longtime employees who had seemed satisfied with their compensation are starting to want a bigger piece of the action.

Maher must decide where he wants Waterway to go and how Carter and the company's compensation structure should figure in Waterway's future. Belatedly, he is realizing that he has neither a marketing strategy nor a clearly articulated business strategy.

Six experts offer real solutions to this fictitious case-study dilemma: James McCann and Kay Henry, two presidents of growing and changing companies; Myra Hart, a business professor and cofounder of a successful growth company; Ronald Rudolph and Bruce Schlegel, a director of human resources and a director of compensation and benefits at the same high-tech company; and Alan Johnson, the director of a consulting firm specializing in compensation issues.

"I'm challenged and motivated where I am, and I like the company. You know that. But I've got to say I'm interested in the opportunity you're describing because of the money and the equity position. For those reasons alone, it's tough to pass by. Let me think about it some more and call you in the morning. Thanks, Les."

That was the extent of the conversation Cyrus Maher, CEO of Waterway Industries, overheard when he came around the corner just outside of Lee Carter's office. She must have been talking with Les Finch, Maher thought. Here's trouble.

Of course, it didn't necessarily mean anything, Maher told himself as he passed the office, waving to Carter. Finch, a well-connected marketing consultant, had been the matchmaker between Carter and Waterway Industries to begin with. With the company in the fourth quarter of its best year ever, he certainly wouldn't be encouraging her to leave. Would he?

Maher got a cup of coffee in the company's first floor kitchenette and deliberately took the long way back to his office, through the design room. As always, the atmosphere was upbeat, but these days he also thought he could detect a sense of purpose that had never before been a part of Waterway's organization.

Maher's friend said kayaks would be the next big trend.

Founded in 1963 in Lake Placid, New York, Waterway had started out as a small, high-quality canoe maker. Over the years, it had built a good reputation all through the Northeast and had acquired a base of customers in the Pacific Northwest as well. By 1982, Waterway was comfortably ensconced in the canoe market nationwide, and it had maintained a steady growth right up until 1990. Then, at the insistence of a friend who was the head of a major dealer and expedition company, Maher had decided to venture into kayaks. His friend had said that kayaks were the next big trend and that Maher would be a fool not to sign on.

Maher had done some checking and found the prospects promising. So by the end of 1992, Waterway had begun selling its own line of compact, inexpensive, high-impact plastic kayaks. Within one quarter, Maher had known that the move had been a smart one. Almost all of Waterway's existing canoe customers—mostly wholesalers who then sold to liveries and sporting goods stores—had placed sizable kayak orders. A number of private-label entities had also inquired about Waterway, and Maher was considering producing private-label kayaks for those companies on a limited basis.

For the most part, the staff had adjusted easily to the company's faster pace. The expanded business hadn't changed Waterway's informal work style, and people seemed to appreciate that. Maher knew that most of his employees were avid outdoor types who viewed their jobs as a means to an end, and he respected that perspective. On days when the weather was particularly good, he knew that the building would be pretty empty by 4 P.M. But he also knew that his employees liked their jobs. Work was always completed on time, and people were outspoken with new ideas and with suggestions for improving current designs and processes. There was no mistaking the genuine camaraderie.

Maher walked through the design room, stopping to talk with one of the two designers and to admire the latest drawings. Then he headed for the administrative suite. His thoughts returned to the company's recent history. Until 1990, Waterway's sales and revenues had increased with the market, and Maher hadn't been motivated to push any harder. But when he had decided to venture

When the weather was good, the building would be empty by 4 P.M.

into kayaking, he also had thought he should gear up marketing—get ready for the big trend if it came. Until then, there had never been a formal, structured marketing department at Waterway. He had thought it was time. That's why he had hired Lee Carter.

Carter had gotten her M.B.A. when she was 31. To do so, she had left a fast-track position in sales at Waterway's major competitor in the canoe market to devote her full attention to her studies. Finch, who was something of a mentor for Carter, had told her that she would hit the ceiling too early in her career if she didn't have the credentials to compete in her field.

In her final term at business school, which had included a full course load plus a demanding internship with the Small Business Administration, Carter had interviewed with Waterway. Finch had called to introduce her, but once Maher had met her and she had begun to outline the ways in which she could improve the company's sales and marketing efforts, Maher had needed no other references. He had thought from the start that Carter might be the right person to nurture the company's interest in the growing kayaking business and to run with it if the sport's popularity really took off.

Maher knew Carter would be good, but she brought in more kayak orders than even he *had expected.*

When it had, he was proved right. True, the market was extremely favorable, but Carter had brought in more orders than even Maher had thought possible. Fortunately, the company had been able to keep up by contracting with other manufacturing companies for more product. Waterway had been extremely effective in keeping inventory in line with customer demand.

Maher was impressed with Carter's performance. From day one, she had been completely focused. She traveled constantly—worked so hard that she barely had time to get to know the staff. She came in on weekends to catch up with paperwork. Along with two of her direct reports, she had even missed the annual Waterway picnic; the three had been on the road, nailing down a large order. It was a dedication—a level of energy—that Maher had never seen before, and he liked what it said about his company.

Back in his office, Maher found that he couldn't concentrate on the product development report in front of him. That bit of conversation he had overheard outside Carter's office was troubling.

He certainly knew about the lucrative packages that were being offered in the sporting goods industry—even in Waterway's niche. He'd even heard that some sales managers were commanding a quarter of a million dollars or more. He had read enough of the annual reports of his publicly traded competitors to know that larger organizations created all sorts of elaborate systems—supplemental retirement packages, golden handcuffs, stock options, deferred compensation arrangements—to hold on to their top performers.

Maher wanted to recognize Carter's contribution. She had been extremely successful in opening new sales channels, and she was personally responsible for 40% of the company's sales for the last two years. Before Carter, the majority of sales had come through the independent reps and distributors. The sales network had grown informally, and Maher had never really tracked it or thought much about building a sales force or developing a formal distribution plan. Those were areas he wanted Carter to concentrate on as director of marketing, but right now she really had her hands full because business was booming.

He thought about the rest of the company. Waterway employed 45 people. Turnover was low; there was hardly ever any grumbling from the ranks. Recently, though, both of his designers had approached him—independently of each other—to request salary adjustments. They had been looking for equity in the company—a cut of the profits if their designs did well. Maher had rejected the proposals but had given the more senior of the two a modest raise and an extra week's vacation and had increased the bonuses of both. They had seemed happy with their new arrangements.

Then there was his former CFO, Chris Papadopoulos, who had left last year to take a position with a power boat manufacturer in Florida. Papadopoulos had twice requested that Maher redesign his compensation package to include equity, and because Maher hadn't been persuaded, Papadopoulos had left for a better job. Waterway's current CFO seemed perfectly content with a base salary and bonus.

The phone rang, jolting Maher out of his thoughts. It was Pat Mason, his assistant, reminding him that his flight to the Watergear Association meeting in Seattle would leave in three hours and that he had things to do before he left.

What Is Fair Pay?

Upon arrival at SeaTac airport, Maher met up with Bryce Holmes, president of Emerald Rafting. Holmes had been a trusted colleague since Maher had entered the business. The two ran into each other frequently at industry and trade shows and tried to get together for a meal at association meetings whenever they could. They took a cab to a seafood restaurant near the Bainbridge Island ferry landing. As always, the conversation centered on the industry.

"Let me ask you this," Maher said, as the waiter served his salmon in white wine and caper sauce. "Do you think that we have to pay our new marketing people more than the industry standard? I mean, when is too much, too much? And who determines the standard anyway? I'd hate to think I would lose a really great marketing manager, but I don't know what to do."

Holmes nodded. "It's tough, because in today's business climate, marketers aren't loyal to one particular industry. Your marketing person would probably be just as happy working in the health club field or for a top-of-the-line jewelry company. Or in speed-boats, for that matter. Or at a phone company. God help you if she gets an offer from the telecommunications industry. The skill is transferable—people go where the money is. And you, my friend, have a reputation for a tight wallet."

"The business could stand to pay more," Maher said, "but I want to avoid the habit of paying now for results down the road."

He said it with a smile, but Maher still grimaced in response. He mentally reviewed his payroll. Professional staffers received a salary and a year-end bonus—10% to 15% of their pay. The controller made $65,000. The office administration manager was pulling $39,000. One designer received $48,000; the other $53,000. Maher himself took $150,000 annually, with a bonus if the company had a good year. And he was paying Carter $51,000 plus a yearly bonus of between $15,000 and $19,000, to make up for not paying a commission on her sales.

"I know the business could stand to pay more," Maher said, "but I don't want to get into the habit of paying now for results down the road. Too many people have gotten into trouble that way."

Holmes held up a warning hand. "I'm just telling you," he said, "that this is something we're all struggling with. I don't want to have to increase compensation costs for the people who seem satisfied now, either. You take someone who is making 60K a year, and you bump them to 85 with a package deal because they get wind of another offer, and what do you have? Not someone who is satisfied, that's for sure. You have someone who doesn't trust you anymore because they thought you were being fair at 60 and evidently you weren't. So now they think they can't trust you at 85. You see what I'm getting at?"

Holmes continued. "We're actually thinking of outsourcing marketing and sales. I'd guess that our pay scales aren't much higher than yours, and it seems that all we've been doing for the last two years is training employees for other companies. And although I shouldn't say this, my friend, I feel that I have to: The rumor mill says that Lee Carter is being tempted to leave Waterway even as we speak."

Maher nodded. "I know that. But, frankly, I'm not sure what to do about it."

More Money, More Growth?

Back in Lake Placid the following Tuesday, Maher had an appointment with Kate Travis, head of the commercial lending department at CenterTrust. Waterway had been doing its banking with CenterTrust for years. Travis showed Maher into her office and got out the company file.

"It looks as though kayaking really did take off," she said, studying the most recent report. "Based on your interim financials, you seem to be on target with your projections. Now, as I understand it, this additional line of credit would be to cover you for accounts receivable, is that correct?"

Maher nodded. "The sales are even better than we had anticipated," he said. "We're outsourcing to a certain extent, but we would also like to gear up production in-house. The increased credit would also give me a chance to look at the forest instead of the trees, if you will."

Travis took notes as they spoke. "Tell me a little bit about your sales," she asked. "What enabled you to do this well? Sales seem to be ahead of your projections."

"In a word, Lee Carter. She's our new marketing department, to put it simply. She's the best hiring decision I've ever made. The market has been agreeable, of course, but without Carter, we wouldn't have been able to take advantage of it."

"I did note that your operating expenses are higher than you had anticipated. Travel and entertainment, in particular."

"A natural outgrowth of our new marketing strategy," Maher said.

Travis continued. "You're also paying out more commissions to your reps and distributors than you ever have before. Now, I know that you have limited your exposure on some costs by outsourcing the manufacturing of certain boat models, but I really think . . ."

"We've also used consultants and temporary employees to handle short-term back-office and accounting support."

"Yes. I wonder if there isn't some more you can do along those lines before reaching for additional credit. Have you analyzed the increase in your sales and marketing costs?"

The two spoke for more than a half an hour, then Travis closed the meeting. "I'll get back in touch with you," she said.

Late that afternoon, Maher tried to finish up the short speech he was planning to deliver at the local Rotary meeting that evening. He couldn't concentrate. His conversation with Travis had raised some doubts in his mind about redesigning Carter's compensation package. With the new line of credit, would he be spreading himself too thin? Suppose he offered Carter a commission arrangement. That might keep her from taking any of those offers being waved in her face right now. But she *would* leave when the kayak boom eventually played out—unless by then Waterway was already pursuing the next hot product market. At the moment, Maher had no idea what that product would be. Chasing fad markets hadn't ever been part of his plan, and although his foray into kayaks was working well for the time being, he had never thought until now that the cutting edge was where he wanted Waterway to be.

Would an even faster pace change Waterway's informal style?

Should Maher give his star performer star rewards—or risk her leaving?

Six experts weigh human resource strategies.

JAMES MCCANN *is the founder and president of 1-800-FLOWERS, based in Westbury, New York.*

Top executives usually don't have the luxury of a clear vision of the future, and Cyrus Maher is no exception. He may not realize it right now, but Maher is at a moment of truth as far as Waterway Industries is concerned. Whatever decisions he makes in the next few days will determine the kind of company he'll be governing over the long term.

Frankly, it's a wonderful position to be in. Maher may decide that he wants to run a sleepy little company— that he doesn't want any more pressure, doesn't want the gun to his head all the time—and that's fine. Or he may decide that he wants to go forward and grow aggressively. That's fine, too. Maher is a lucky man. In some industries, he wouldn't have such choices. The market would demand that he grow the company, sell it, or fold. Here, it is largely up to him what happens to his career and to his company.

But Maher does not have unlimited time in which to make his decision. In fact, if he doesn't act soon, his inaction, his employees, and the market will decide the future course of Waterways for him. He is doing the right things—asking colleagues and friends what they think of his strategy, management style, and market position— but he needs to do the right things a little faster, with a decision point in mind.

Going forward is a little scarier than going backward, but I suspect that Maher wouldn't be happy if Waterways returned to the sleepy little company it once was. So for the purposes of discussion, let's say that he decides to grow the company. In such a scenario, the most important thing for him to keep in mind is that he is, first and foremost, a cultural engineer. Every action he takes will affect the culture of the company, and it's up to him to create and maintain the kind of culture he wants to have.

Take his compensation plan—the most immediate critical item he must face once he commits to moving ahead. The kind of pay plans that most people considered normal in the past—base salaries with annual step increases in pay across the board—don't exist anymore. We're part of a new entrepreneurial environment, and the old rules don't apply. It is increasingly more acceptable to receive equity as part of a compensation package, depending on your level. And that equity is often in lieu of more generous cash compensation. It's also socially acceptable—and increasingly common—to be a hired gun, a specialist brought in at a higher rate for a single purpose. Maher needs to address this new environment when he makes a decision about Lee Carter's arrangement. But that doesn't mean he needs to create the same kind of compensation package for all his other employees.

Maher should take what I call the "Neon Deion" approach (after star National Football League player Deion Sanders). Jerry Jones, owner of the Dallas Cowboys, knows that his core team members are important, and he values them. But he also makes them understand that in order for the organization to be successful, he has to buy one extra ingredient, the hired gun, the star cornerback. He has to make two points clear: first, that he knows that the extra ingredient costs more because of market demands; second, that paying the extra money for Sanders doesn't mean he doesn't value the core.

Maher has to develop an understanding of what his people want. Carter and the two designers may want equity in the company, but that doesn't mean that everyone is going to want it. What good is equity if you want to buy a house and you need a mortgage?

I'd like to see Waterway take the cafeteria approach to compensation—at least until the company settles into its new pace. That is, I'd like to see Maher offering a variety of options to his employees. He can pay a base salary—as set by industry and community standards. And then he can offer extras based on how the company does. Those extras can take the form of equity or cash, depending on what individual employees value more highly.

Regardless of whether Maher decides to grow Waterway or take it gradually back down to the kind of company it used to be, he must talk to Carter as soon as he has made the decision. In fact, that's another reason for deciding fast. Carter will be coming to talk to him sooner rather than later, and if he beats her to the punch, he'll be in a much better position to get some honest feedback and support from her.

Maher should realize that Carter, being on the road almost all the time, is probably suffering from the road warrior blues. When people are working tremendously hard and traveling constantly, they can feel euphoric. At 1-800-FLOWERS, we feel that way during the flower holidays—our busiest times. But when the rush is over, it is normal to be exhausted and a little blue. When Carter is at her home office, she may be thinking, "Am I really appreciated? Does anyone care that I work so hard?" If she is unable to answer those questions with a yes, it is only a matter of time before she accepts an offer from another company.

Maher needs to get to her before that happens and show her that he is willing to create the kind of social structure that she needs in order to feel accepted— whether she is the key to Waterway's growth or simply a good marketing executive riding a trend. If she's too busy to attend the company picnic, he needs to find another way for the company to get to know her better. She needs to know that the company is cheering for her, not resentful of her or simply ignorant of her activities. She'll be able to help Maher figure this out; it's pretty clear that she likes the company and would prefer to stay there. But if he doesn't let her know that he understands her position and wants to make everything work out, she will accept another offer.

Right now, Waterway is on the verge of enjoying its 15 minutes of fame. My own company is in the middle of that 15 minutes, and although I can tell you that it is tremendously exciting, it is not impressive in and of itself. What will impress *me* is if I'm still being tapped for speaking and writing engagements in ten years—if 1-800-FLOWERS has created a culture that maintains the excitement and commitment we currently have. Maher should strive for similar goals. He's in a good position now, but regardless of the path he chooses, what matters is the foundation he creates for the future.

KAY HENRY *is the president of Mad River Canoe, a company based in Waitsfield, Vermont.*

Maher needs Carter at the moment for one very simple reason: he doesn't have anyone to replace her. From a long-term perspective, he is unlikely to keep Carter. His business is more about lifestyle choice and a love of the product than it is about money, and Carter doesn't seem to be in love with the lifestyle or the products that Waterway can offer. But for the short term, I think Maher will be able to hold her if he changes her compensation package, perhaps by offering her a commission arrangement.

Carter is the only semblance of organized marketing that Waterway has ever seen. Maher should take advantage of her energy while she's there. But he shouldn't let her continue to focus solely on sales. Her performance has been great, but what he really needs is for her to build a marketing department and work on a marketing strategy. I'm amazed that the company has gotten this far without a formal marketing plan; it certainly won't be able to get much further without one. Too much has happened too fast for the company to continue to play marketing by ear.

Before Carter develops a marketing plan, however, Maher should really do some hard thinking about where he wants the company to go. If he does want to pursue other trendy product lines, he may have to bring in a partner or give employees a stake in the company. That would be a big change for him, but to be honest, I don't think that he has the stamina to lead the company into aggressive growth by himself. He just doesn't seem to be the type; I certainly can't picture him missing a company picnic! For that reason, I think he should also consider pulling back and taking the company small again. Is growth what he really wants, or is he just fascinated by something new that won't make him happy over the long term?

He should work closely with Carter as she builds the marketing department. If she builds a team that suits her and then leaves to pursue a fast-paced career in software sales, he may find himself at odds with the personalities she has assembled. Right now, Carter's energetic style is intriguing. But if it simply isn't Maher, then he will have a hard time living and working with it over time.

For now, I don't think that Maher should worry too much about giving equity stakes to his employees across the board. Offering his designers a royalty arrangement is probably a good idea, but equity stakes would be a big jump for him, and they might not crack up to be all that the employees think they should be. Waterway is not an unusual example of a small, focused sporting goods company. Employees don't have to be part of the business by owning stock. They are a part of the business because they enjoy the lifestyle it offers them and because they take pride in the kinds of products they make—and the kinds of experiences that the products make possible for customers.

What Maher needs to do is to remind his employees of that fact. They have an excellent culture right now. They have benefits that other, fast-paced companies cannot offer. If equity offerings are tied up with growing the company, then the culture will inevitably change—and fast.

Of course, Maher may eventually decide to offer equity anyway, but in a different context. Over the next few years, he should be thinking about retiring. With the exception of Carter (who is a star, but probably not a good fit), he seems to have assembled a group of people who are not only bright but also devoted to the water-sports business. If he gets these people to invest in the company and to take it forward with a clear vision in mind, he will have left a legacy to be proud of.

MYRA HART *is a founder of Staples, based in Framing-ham, Massachusetts, and is an assistant professor at the Harvard Business School in Boston, Massachusetts.*

For Maher, trying to resolve salary, bonus, equity, and profit sharing issues without testing his own assumptions about Waterway would rank somewhere between foolhardy and disastrous. First, he needs to review his company's history and think hard about his goals.

When he began the business in 1963, Maher had a set of product, profitability, and personal lifestyle objectives. Building a quality canoe was most likely a choice that grew out of a love of canoeing, a unique knowledge of the requisite performance criteria, and a vision of design and manufacturing processes that could deliver a superior product. It took him nearly 20 years to build Waterway's brand franchise, and once he achieved that, he let the industry set the pace of the company's growth. He was not particularly aggressive in the canoe market, nor did he explore related opportunities. He seemed content with business as usual and time left over for play.

What changed? How much of his 1990 expansion into kayaks was a conscious decision to seek new opportunity? How much was prompted by a perceived slackening in canoes? Was he becoming bored with the status quo or simply responding to a dealer's request? Did he have any idea of the challenges that he might face if the business experienced a serious change of pace?

If Maher is satisfied that growth was—and still is—the right decision, then he needs to go on to the next set of questions: Was the choice of the kayak business the best way to achieve growth? How well is it working? The kayak line seemed logical at the time he first considered it, and four years later, the strategy seems to have proved its value. But does Maher have a clear understanding of how kayak sales may be affecting his canoe business? Is there synergy between the product lines, or does the fact that sales are being made to the same customer base suggest that there may be some erosion of the canoe sales? How many new outlets have been added to the Waterway roster? At what cost? How healthy are the margins?

Has Maher considered any nonfinancial costs brought about by the introduction of the kayak line? If Carter is personally capturing 40% of the new sales, is she crowding out the existing sales network, possibly eroding their interest in the canoe line or driving up the sales commission they demand for handling the smaller accounts?

What about the manufacturing side of the business? So far, Maher has dealt with increased demand by outsourcing some of the production, but he is currently thinking about expanding Waterway's capacity and tak-

ing on some private-label manufacturing. Further, he is
looking ahead to the day when the kayak business slack-
ens and wondering what the next hot product will be.
Can he really have thought through the ramifications of
increased fixed costs and contract manufacturing when
he is unsure of future demand?

If, after a careful analysis, Maher finds that he is still
committed to continuing his growth strategy, he needs
to review how well the organization has adapted to
growth to date and where it is showing signs of stress.
There are some indicators that the implicit work/play
contract may be changing and, with it, the perception
that the compensation is fair. The designers may believe
that they are contributing more to the company's bottom line now and that they should share in the profits.
Whether they have expanded their skill sets or have simply found themselves in more demand in a more competitive industry, some Waterway employees believe that
they are worth more now. It may be that they have better
information and are making comparisons across the
industry but are not accounting for some of the perks
that they still get. Maher needs to do some homework to
understand what is behind the requests for compensation adjustments.

If he concludes that some change in the Waterway
compensation package is appropriate, Maher needs to
consider the organizational implications. Changes made
as an exception for one member of the staff will be perceived as inequitable and eventually will be divisive.
Maher seems to know this, but he also seems unsure of
which alternative—higher base pay, commissions, equity
across the board—he should pursue. His employees' proposals to increase base pay and to participate in equity
ownership are merely their approximations of fair

compensation and of how to participate in the business's growth. The suggestions need not be taken literally.

I would advise Maher to think twice before offering equity to anyone. Although often considered a panacea for aligning employees' and owners' interests, it may fall far short of Waterway employees' expectations and cause substantial headaches for Maher.

Since Maher has not given any indication that he is considering a sale of the business in either the public or private markets, there is no obvious way for an employee to extract equity value from the company at will. And even if Maher were to offer equity, a growth strategy would demand reinvestment in the company rather than distribution of profits to shareholders. His employees would probably be frustrated with their lack of liquidity and the long delay in sharing profits.

For his part, Maher might be equally frustrated by the challenges of sharing ownership in his privately held company. Among those challenges would be setting and adjusting prices or valuation for shares to be distributed. If Maher opts to set up a stock repurchase plan for departing employees, he may actually provide an incentive to leave rather than to stay. He could also be very frustrated by having minority shareholders who want a voice in decision making. On a more technical note, if Waterway is a Subchapter S Corporation, Maher will be forced to choose between limiting the number of shareholders to 35 or changing the legal form of the organization.

A profit-sharing plan for the existing private company can achieve the goals of the employees more simply and will allow them to reap rewards as they are earned. Some form of bonus plan that recognizes and rewards individual achievements can be coupled with profit sharing to provide a blended compensation package. As for base pay, Maher needs to look at trends in his industry and be sure that the package he is offering is equitable. He should consider all the benefits Waterway provides, including time off for kayaking and canoeing as well as more tangible benefits. Finally, he needs to factor cost-of-living adjustments into his plan. Waterway is still a small business in an upstate New York community that appears to draw primarily on the local population for its employees. It does not appear that base pay is far off the mark, but there is a need to provide incentives and rewards for employees willing and able to make the changes that growth demands.

When Maher is comfortable with the appropriate salary and benefit ranges for the various positions, he should run through the financial implications for the business. Once he has done his own reality check on the anticipated adjustment, he should involve his employees in the process. Allowing key employees to consider acceptable options and make recommendations may be enormously helpful. (Actually, although the issue of succession planning wasn't mentioned in the case study, Maher better be thinking hard about that, too. If he has been with the company since the early 1960s, he should be thinking about when and how he plans to retire. Is there a likely successor currently working for Waterway? If so, shouldn't that person have input into the decisions Maher is facing?)

Maher needs to weigh whether or not Lee Carter should be at the top of the list of Waterway's key employees. Carter was brought in to manage marketing, but so far, she seems to have spent very little time building a marketing organization. She has fallen back on her old skills as a salesperson and has spent the majority of her time on the road. In fact, she and her two assistants have not spent much time acclimating to the existing Waterway culture, let alone trying to develop new systems. Carter would probably be far more effective if she got off the road at least two or three days a week and began working on marketing plans and sales force management.

Carter's loss to another organization, whether to a direct competitor or to a company in another industry, would have an immediate impact on Waterway's sales. However, the relationships with the wholesalers are in place, and there is a network of independent sales reps who could service most of her accounts if she left. (As an aside, my own instinct would have been to talk with Carter and let her know that I had inadvertently overheard her conversation. Such a course would have had the advantage of allowing me to assess the intensity of the immediate threat and to determine how much urgency was required. It would certainly have provided some valuable information and probably would have bought me some time if Carter wasn't actually planning to leave. But such action doesn't seem to fit in with Maher's personal style.)

Maher has done a lot of thinking and has talked with trusted colleagues and advisors. With a review of his objectives, an understanding of current strengths and weaknesses, a clearer picture of where he wants to take Waterway, and a realistic appraisal of his current staff, he'll be ready to make some decisions. Then he can sit down with Carter and find out how and where she wants to fit in.

RONALD RUDOLPH *is the director of human resources at 3Com Corporation in Santa Clara, California, and* BRUCE SCHLEGEL *is the director of compensation and benefits at 3Com.*

Maher has gotten himself into a potential no-win situation because he lacks a clear business strategy. A company's business strategy should drive its compensation plan, and in the absence of either, Maher has been forced to react emotionally and inconsistently to employees' demands. He has already lost at least one senior manager that we know of, and he runs a great risk of having more key people lured away to greener pastures. Unfortunately, Maher's situation will only get worse if he chooses to pursue new markets and accelerated growth—unless he gets a handle on exactly what he wants the new Waterway to look like and makes a couple of important decisions accordingly.

The successful compensation and rewards techniques that Maher used in the past, when Waterway was enjoying steady but modest growth, are less successful in a fast-growth environment. It's no surprise that the traditional Waterway employee, who treasures the informality and camaraderie of the organization, is demanding to share in the tangible rewards of the more successful company. And the kinds of new employees that Waterway may need for future success—people with special advanced business skills, who may not necessarily share a love of the outdoors or a passion for Waterway's products—are certainly not going to be happy with outmoded compensation offerings.

If Maher wants to pursue Waterway's opportunity for accelerated growth, he needs a formal compensation philosophy and strategy—based on his business plan—to serve as an anchor for making compensation decisions in the new environment. Having said that, we should point out that Maher is not necessarily faced with an all-or-nothing scenario. He does not have to change his company's culture completely in order to succeed. Answering the following questions may help him figure out what needs to change and what needs to stay the same.

- **Where does Maher want to position the company in the market?** One option would be to adopt a market-priced philosophy to let the marketplace determine the value of a particular set of skills. The market may value design skills in the new or so-called fad product areas much more highly than it does those related to older products. With a market-priced philosophy and a stated business goal of expanding quickly into new markets with cutting-edge products, Waterway would compensate at or above the competition to get and retain top design talent. Another option would be to price jobs under competitive rates, with the stated goal of attracting and retaining talented people who value a flexible work environment that encourages outdoor pursuits.

- **How should noncash compensation and rewards fit into Waterway's business strategy?** Noncash rewards are a key component of a successful compensation strategy regardless of whether Maher sets pay at or below the market rate. But they are especially critical if he goes with the latter approach. If a high-growth company decides to pay below market rate, it must reward employees in some other tangible way for their contributions to company success. Profit sharing is one alternative. Another, easier way to keep people committed and use no cash (bankers love this!) is to offer equity. Performance-based equity sharing is an effective way of rewarding and retaining key employees. But there are other options as well, including recognition awards (cash or in kind) and personal development accounts for training and development programs (in addition to tuition reimbursement programs). Whatever they are, they should support the business plan, be consistent with the compensation philosophy, create an effective economic partnership between employee and employer, and take into consideration the competition's offerings and the broader external job market.

- **Which skills must be retained internally, and which can be outsourced?** Are creating proprietary product designs and innovating to allow rapid penetration into new markets the competencies that the company must nurture for growth consistent with the business plan? Are people with these abilities more or less likely to value the intangibles of Waterway's environment than, say, sales-oriented people, who may be more motivated by cash compensation tied directly to sales? Maher is impressed with Carter's performance; but in his current situation, he should put his energy into assessing the distribution strategy in the context of an aggressive business plan rather than react too quickly to the possibility of losing one lone ranger, albeit a highly successful marketing person. Perhaps sales, marketing, and distribution ability could be more efficiently and effectively outsourced than developed and managed in-house.

Those questions raise issues that are central to any compensation strategy, and Waterway needs a strategy—fast. The new strategy doesn't necessarily have to include higher wages or be inconsistent with Waterway's superior work environment, the value of which should not be underestimated. Such an environment can continue to be a key employee motivator and contribute immeasurably to loyalty, high morale, and productivity.

In fact, behavioral scientists have shown repeatedly that people are not motivated directly by pay but that pay becomes a dissatisfier when other elements of the satisfaction formula are lacking or out of kilter. But if Maher stays on the same growth path without adjusting his strategy, that superior environment is going to erode anyway. The only way Maher is going to get out of his current predicament is to define his new business goals clearly and then define a compensation philosophy and strategy that explicitly supports those goals.

ALAN JOHNSON *is the managing director of Johnson Associates, a New York–based consulting firm specializing in compensation issues.*

Overhearing Carter's conversation with Les Finch was the best thing that could have happened to Maher and perhaps to Waterway Industries. Not only did it get Maher thinking about what Carter has meant to the company's phenomenal growth, it gave him a much-needed reason to consider the importance and needs of Waterway's other employees. Waterway needs Carter—at least in the short term. So any intellectual discussion of whether or not Maher should rethink her compensation arrangement is pointless. From a business standpoint, Maher has only one reasonable choice. Otherwise, Waterway's kayak business will sink and employee morale will suffer.

Granted, Maher doesn't seem to have a clear sense of what he intends to do with his business. But changing Carter's compensation arrangement will buy him some time to make those important strategic decisions. By pacifying Carter now, he can maintain his marketing and sales engine. He can then maximize the kayak boom and use that time to consider whether he wants to continue to grow the company. If he decides that the kayak boom will be the end and that he wants Waterway to return to its former state, he can wind down the marketing effort and phase out his part-timers and his outsourcing arrangements over a two- or three-year period. Maher isn't a snap-to-it kind of guy. It took him two or three years to get fully invested in the kayak market; there's no reason why he can't take the same amount of time to phase out of it.

As a short-term incentive, Maher should offer Carter a stay-put bonus or phantom shares in the business, contingent on a commitment for a given period of time. Then if Maher decides to pursue an aggressive growth strategy, he can offer her a three-to-five-year performance-based cash incentive plan. Her annual incentive might be based on her sales volume and on her ability to control marketing costs as a percentage of sales. In either case, he should ensure that Carter's base salary is competitive by checking it against available market data and running it past other marketing people he knows. (He can also check any one of a number of annually published salary surveys.) If her salary is not competitive, then an immediate adjustment is in order.

Maher also needs to consider other key employees. Regardless of the business strategy he eventually settles on, an equity arrangement for other senior staff will help focus the company; it will also provide a retention incentive. He may be concerned about such a move, but he should think about it this way: Would he rather own 100% of a little or 80% of a lot? If Maher doesn't give up some equity, he may find himself with much less of a company than he had to begin with—in terms of size and quality of life. Maher is the one who started the company on its current path. To put the brakes on without any consideration for the change it has already undergone would be disastrous.

Once he has given his top managers equity in the company, Maher should solicit their advice about whether and how Waterway should grow. Most of Waterway's senior managers will probably be on the same wavelength. They joined Waterway because of its culture and its business, not because it was a big money-maker. But different perspectives—such as Carter's—can help Maher grow the company, take it public, or shrink it in a healthy, well-rounded way.

Throughout all of this, Maher must communicate with his other employees. I'm sure that there are rumors going around right now that the company culture is going to change. If Maher is holding Carter up as an example of a great employee, his other staff members are probably wondering how they can keep up or whether they even want to. Maher needs to allay their fears, but he also needs to let them know what he is thinking about. If, along with the management team, he decides to pursue a growth strategy—even a modest one—he should let his employees know exactly what that will mean for them. If he institutes a companywide bonus plan, he needs to be candid about what that means for Waterway's culture. If he expects people to put in longer hours, he has to say so. And if they express concerns, he must be ready to respond.

For example, if one of his employees says, "Look, I know the workday ends at 5, but I always pick up my children from day care at 4," Maher needs to be prepared to react honestly. I suspect that he will be able to say that he is committed to managing the new company expectations in a fair way. He may explain that the push for more hours will be a seasonal kind of thing or that if people want to leave at 4 p.m., he expects them to put in more hours at another time. If Maher promises no surprises and keeps that promise, he'll also keep the loyalty and respect of his staff, without which Waterway would sink.

Originally published in July–August 1996
Reprint 96408

About the Contributors

At the time this article was originally published, JOHN CASE was the author of *Open-Book Management* and *The Open-Book Experience*, as well as several other business books.

BRIAN J. HALL is Associate Professor of Business Administration at Harvard Business School. Previously, he was Assistant Professor of Economics in the Harvard Economics Department, and served on the staff of the President's Council of Economic Advisers. Professor Hall's research focuses on the intersection of corporate governance and finance, and executive compensation and incentives. He has published in a variety of academic and practitioner-oriented journals, including *American Economic Review*, *Quarterly Journal of Economics*, and *Harvard Business Review*. His research has been cited frequently in the national and international financial press, including features in *BusinessWeek*, *Red Herring*, and the News Hour with Jim Lehrer, and he has been the featured speaker at numerous conferences and symposia. Professor Hall is the recipient of several teaching prizes, including the Harvard college-wide 1997 Phi Beta Kappa Prize for excellence in teaching. He is currently a member of the Global Corporate Governance Inititative and the Human Resource Initiative at the

Harvard Business School. Professor Hall is a Faculty Research Fellow at the National Bureau of Economic Research and is the Berol Faculty Fellow at the Harvard Business School. He has consulted with and advised many companies in the area of the stock option and incentive strategy, including Merck, McKinsey, Towers Perrin, and iQuantic.

ALFIE KOHN has been described as the country's leading critic of competition, although he is quick to point out that there is not much competition for that title. He is the author of eight books and scores of articles on human behavior, management, and education. His best-known books are *Punished by Rewards* and *No Contest*. Mr. Kohn lives (actually) in Belmont, Massachusetts, and (virtually) at www.alfiekohn.org.

At the time this article was originally published, ROBERT D. NICOSON was the Director of Human Resources for the Pioneer Group, a financial services and natural resources company based in Boston, Massachusetts. He was responsible for all domestic and international human-resources services, including executive compensation design and administration.

JEFFREY PFEFFER is the Thomas D. Dee II Professor of Organizational Behavior at the Stanford University Graduate School of Business, where he has taught since 1979. Dr. Pfeffer has served on the faculties at the University of Illinois, the University of California at Berkeley, and the Harvard Business School. He has taught executive seminars in twenty-six countries throughout the world and is the Former Director of Executive Education at Stanford. He serves on the board of directors of Actify, Audible Magic, Portola Packaging, SonoSite, and

Unicru, as well as on numerous editorial boards of scholarly journals. He is the author of *The Human Equation, New Directions for Organizational Theory, Competitive Advantage Through People, Managing with Power, Organizations and Organization Theory, Power in Organizations,* and *Organizational Design,* and coauthor of *Hidden Value, The Knowing-Doing Gap,* and *The External Control of Organizations,* as well as over 100 articles and book chapters.

ALFRED RAPPAPORT is the Leonard Spacek Professor Emeritus at Northwestern University's J.L. Kellog Graduate School of Management, where he was a member of the faculty for 28 years. He is also Shareholder Value Advisor to L.E.K. Consulting and author of the widely acclaimed book, *Creating Shareholder Value.* His most recent book, *Expectations Investing,* was coauthored with Michael J. Mauboussin. Dr. Rappaport is the author of over seventy articles focusing primarily on applying shareholder value methodology to planning, performance evaluation, incentive compensation, mergers and acquisitions, and corporate governance issues. He has been a guest columnist for the *Wall Street Journal,* the *New York Times,* and *Business Week.* He also created and designed the annually published *Wall Street Journal Shareholder Scoreboard,* a ranking by total shareholder returns of the 1,000 most valuable U.S. corporations.

EGON ZEHNDER is the Chairman of the Board at Egon Zehnder International Inc., one of the largest global executive search firms in the world, which specializes in executive search, management appraisals, and corporate governance appointments. Prior to opening Egon Zehnder International, Mr. Zehnder was with McCann-Erickson in New York and Dusseldorf and Vice President of McCann Erickson Europe, based in Geneva. He is a Member of the Board of Zurich University's Executive Development Institute; Member of the Board of Trustees, IMD (Institute for Management Development), Lausanne, Switzerland; and Chairman of the Nominations Committee of the Swiss-American Chamber of Commerce.

Index